SUCCESSFUL LISTENING

Speech Communication Series

Partial list of books in the Speech Communication Series

Benjamin: *Communication: Concepts and Contexts*

Hauser: *Introduction to Rhetorical Theory*

Kelly/Watson: *Speaking with Confidence and Skill*

Kougl: *Primer for Public Speaking*

Roach/Wyatt: *Successful Listening*

Skopec: *Situational Interviewing*

Thompson: *Communication for Health Professionals*

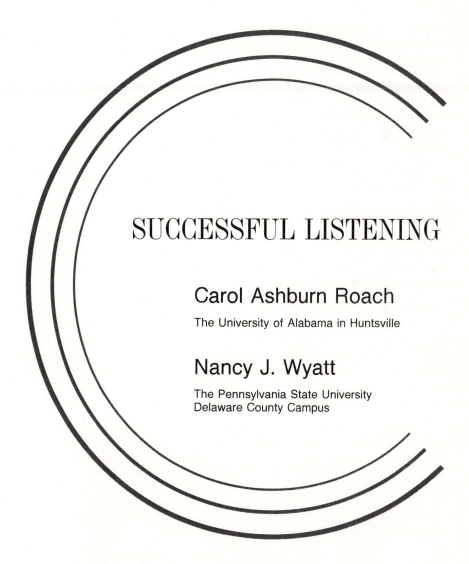

SUCCESSFUL LISTENING

Carol Ashburn Roach

The University of Alabama in Huntsville

Nancy J. Wyatt

The Pennsylvania State University
Delaware County Campus

HARPER & ROW, PUBLISHERS, New York

Cambridge, Philadelphia, San Francisco, Washington,
London, Mexico City, São Paulo, Singapore, Sydney

1817

Sponsoring Editor: Marianne Russell
Project Editor: B. Pelner
Cover Design: Jack Ribik
Text Art: Volt Information Sciences, Inc.
Production Manager: Jeanie Berke
Production Assistant: Paula Roppolo
Compositor: ComCom Division of Haddon Craftsmen, Inc.
Printer and Binder: R. R. Donnelley & Sons Company
Cover Printer: Lynn Art Offset Corporation

Successful Listening

Copyright © 1988 by Harper & Row, Publishers, Inc.

Library of Congress Cataloging in Publication Data

Roach, Carol Ashburn.
  Successful listening / Carol Ashburn Roach, Nancy Wyatt.
    p. cm.
  Includes bibliographies and index.
  ISBN 0-06-045439-3
  1. Listening. I. Wyatt, Nancy. II. Title.
  BR323.L5R62 1988   87-18438
  153.6—dc19   CIP

87 88 89 90 9 8 7 6 5 4 3 2 1

To Gerald M. Phillips

The pursuit of knowledge is a vast cooperative exercise, the most exhilarating and important human aspiration. We all owe a great debt to those who struggled before us to understand the world and shape the ideas that govern our lives. Your example has been an important influence on our own pursuit of knowledge, and we acknowledge our debt to your scholarship.

Contents

Preface

Listening is a topic that seems sadly neglected in the educational process. In school we learn to read and write and sometimes to give speeches, but seldom do we get any formal training in how to listen. Teachers and parents can often be heard admonishing young people to "Pay attention!" and "Listen carefully!" but they never say exactly how to do that. Because we can't actually *see* someone listening, it's hard to put a finger on exactly what someone *does* when he or she is listening. This book is designed to do exactly that—to explain to students what to do in order to listen well. Because we can't see someone listening, we seem to assume that listening is a passive process, something that somehow "gets done" rather than an active process that people have to work at. Nothing could be farther from the truth. Listening is, in fact, hard work, and you have to know what you're doing to be a good listener. Hearing is a natural process, but listening is not.

We believe that listeners who understand the physical and mental processes involved in good listening can learn how to listen more effectively. By more effectively, we mean that listeners will be able to achieve their own listening goals. Listening, like speaking, is a goal-oriented activity. You have to know what you're listening for if you want to do it well. In accordance with this belief, this book takes a rhetorical approach to the study and practice of listening. Listening is analyzed as a communication situation involving people who have specific goals, negotiating with one another to achieve those goals. For centuries rhetoric has been the study of how to speak well; we have just turned the process around and made it also the process of how to listen well.

In accordance with this approach, the book is divided into seven chapters. Each chapter includes specific behavioral goals, explanations of how to achieve those goals, suggested activities for practicing the appropriate listening skills, and recommended readings for further understanding. Within each chapter relevant concepts are illustrated by excerpts from real conversations or stories from real life. Although the book is written with a college classroom in mind, others outside the classroom will find the examples and ideas useful to them in their work and personal lives.

Chapter 1, "Listening and the Rhetorical Process," describes common misconceptions about listening and explains the rhetorical process. Many people mistakenly believe that listening is a natural process that needs no practice, that listening is passive, and that they are good listeners "when they really try." Evidence from studies indicates that none of these beliefs is true. Readers will learn about the rhetorical process of choosing an appropriate goal, analyzing the situation and the speakers, selecting a listening strategy, and evaluating their own performance.

Chapter 2, "What Listening Is—Physical and Psychological Process," illustrates the important differences between hearing and listening. A description of how mechanical sound waves are turned into meaningful information in the brain and how listeners' expectations and assumptions affect that process is included. By the end of the chapter, readers should be able to list and explain several physical, social, and psychological factors that interfere in the process of listening and cause people to misunderstand what they hear.

Chapter 3, "Setting Goals for Listening," explains the four main listening goals: listening to enjoy, to understand, to maintain relationships, and to decide. Then, the process by which readers can learn to set appropriate listening goals for themselves is described. Readers will learn how to recognize a good listening goal and how to make sure they have chosen a goal appropriate for the situation.

Chapter 4, "Listening for Understanding," deals specifically with the process of listening to gather information. Included is an explanation of the importance of context, feelings, word order, and silence to understand what the speaker *means* as opposed to what he or she *says*. Specific advice is offered on how to take account of these four factors to ensure that what listeners hear is what speakers meant them to hear. The authors deal with such topics as emotional responses, personal biases, and nonverbal communication in explaining how to avoid misunderstandings. Common organization patterns are explained and readers are taught how to identify each.

Chapter 5, "Listening to Maintain Relationships," focuses on the personal aspects of listening and how important listening is to getting along with friends and coworkers. Different kinds of listening appropriate for different kinds of relationships are identified, and explanations are provided for listening in each situation. Readers will learn what "dual perspective" is and how to look at the situation from the other person's point of view. The importance of operational definitions is discussed.

Chapter 6, "Listening to Decide," deals with how to listen to people who are trying to persuade you, the process of critical listening, and distinguishing rational from emotional appeals. Several common emotional appeals are identified and discussed. Rational argument is also explained and readers are introduced to common reasoning patterns and forms of evidence. Readers are also introduced to some common propaganda appeals and are given some criteria to use in judging whether the speaker is an expert or not.

Chapter 7, "Listening to Enjoy," focuses on listening to music and oral literature. The three levels of listening to enjoy: the physical level of sensation, the mental level of ideas, and the level of technical expertise are included. Readers are introduced to literary and musical concepts that explain how we can listen on any or all of these levels, depending on why and when we are listening. The chapter ends with an extended example of listening to *The Pirates of Penzance* on all three levels.

We wish to thank many people who have contributed ideas and advice for this book. First, we want to thank our students, families, and colleagues who have served as models and examples in the book. Second, we want to thank the people who read and critiqued the book. A good book is a dialogue, not an individual effort, and we want to acknowledge their contributions. H. Lloyd Goodall, Mary Helen Brown, and Richard Shaw contributed important comments and advice. We also want to thank the reviewers who put in hours of careful thought and recommendations that strengthened the book enormously: Dr. Mary Bozik, University of Northern Iowa, Dr. Ella Erway, Southern Connecticut State University, and Dr. Larry Barker, Auburn University. Finally we want to thank the person who kept our noses to the grindstone and our shoulders to the wheel and expected us to work in that ridiculous position—Gerald M. Phillips, Series Advisor for the Speech Communication Series.

Carol A. Roach
Nancy J. Wyatt

chapter *1*

Listening and the Rhetorical Process

When you have finished this chapter you should be able to:

1. Identify and explain three common misconceptions about listening.
2. Describe the four steps of the rhetorical process.
3. List four possible listening goals.

When you have finished this chapter you should be able to define these important concepts:

1. rhetorical process
2. speaking and listening goals
3. strategies
4. dual perspective

Most texts on listening begin by establishing that listening skills are important to you in school, on the job, and in your personal relationships. Then they go on to convince you that you're not a very good listener. While these two observations may be true, we believe that you already know you could benefit by improving your listening skills or you wouldn't be taking this course. We will not, therefore, bore you by telling you what you already know. Instead, we will introduce you to some common misconceptions about listening and refute those misconceptions. In the process of this discussion, we will show you how improving your listening skills will benefit you, as already mentioned. We will also outline a rhetorical process that will guide you to better listening practices. In addition, we will explain how speaking and listening are not separate activities; in fact, they are both components of an activity we call "communication." By learning to listen better, you will also be learning how to speak better.

MISCONCEPTION NUMBER ONE: LISTENING IS NATURAL

The misconception that listening is natural arises partly because we confuse the process of listening with the process of hearing. Hearing is certainly a natural process. Unless you have organic damage to some part of your ear, you will have been hearing since before you were born. Hearing is a matter of perception of small changes in atmospheric pressure, which goes on continuously, even when you are sleeping. How else would the alarm wake you in the morning? The process of hearing will be considered in some detail in the next chapter. For the present it's enough to distinguish hearing from listening in order to illustrate that listening is not a natural process at all.

Humans can "hear" changes in air pressure in an effective range of frequencies from 20 to 20,000 cycles per second. Changes in air pressure impact the eardrum and are transmitted through the middle ear to the inner ear, where they are transformed into electrochemical messages and sent to the hearing center in the brain. That process is natural and automatic and outside conscious control. Problems start when we confuse this purely automatic physical process with the consciously purposeful psychological process of listening.

Listening is largely a process of discriminating and identifying which sounds are meaningful or important to us and which aren't. We actually focus our hearing in the same way we focus our sight. You can probably remember a time when you didn't "see" something that was in plain sight. Maybe you even fell over it. You have probably also had the experience of talking to someone—a parent, a teacher, a colleague, even a friend—who was thinking about something else and didn't "hear" what you said. In fact, they did hear in the sense that the sounds reached their ears, but they didn't hear what you said because they were paying attention to something else at the time. If you're sufficiently candid, you may also remember some times when you didn't hear something that was said to you because you weren't paying attention. We are all guilty of thinking about other things sometimes. The point is, you did hear, but you weren't listening.

> "Excuse me, Dr. Simpson, I'm having trouble thinking of a good attention getter for my speech."
>
> "What's your topic?"
>
> "I'm talking about Cambodia and the Khmer Rouge, all that killing."
>
> "In that case why don't you use the technique I just illustrated in class, the one from the acid rain speech?"
>
> "I didn't hear that one. I guess I wasn't listening."

The importance of distinguishing between hearing and listening is that we don't need training to hear well, but we do need training to listen well. In fact, if the hearing mechanism is damaged, no amount of training will improve its function. Real deafness can't be cured by trying harder. Faulty listening, on the other hand, can't be cured by medical science or by magic. To learn to listen more effectively, you have to try harder. You have to learn how to listen.

The idea that we learn to listen as children is partially true. Before they start to school, children learn many things by listening. But they only learn as well as they were trained. Unfortunately most of the training children receive in listening skills comes largely in the form of injunctions. "Now, you listen to me!" they are told, or "Listen carefully!" The usefulness of such training can be illustrated by comparing it to a similar injunction to a child to "Catch the ball!" Not very useful advice. It's more useful to show children how to hold their hands and tell them to keep their eyes on the ball. Then give them plenty of supervised practice and explain to them what they are doing right and what they're doing wrong, so they can improve. Without supervised practice, children can pick up bad habits of listening which serve them indifferently as they grow up. Learning to listen is a matter of training; it doesn't come naturally any more than playing ball does.

In one very interesting study, Nichols and Stevens (1957) found evidence that younger children listen better than older children. When the researchers stopped teachers in the middle of lectures and asked the students what the teachers were talking about, they found that 90 percent of the first graders could answer correctly, 80 percent of the second graders could answer correctly, but only 28 percent of the senior high school students could answer correctly. These results might even lead us to believe that we become worse listeners as we grow up. Far from being a natural process, listening is clearly a consciously purposive activity for which we need systematic training and supervision to learn to do well.

Another way to look at listening is as one part of the communication process, like speaking. While we could agree that speaking is a natural human function, no one could deny that children have to be taught how to speak. Certainly no one was born speaking standard English. If you have forgotten the process of learning to speak, spend a couple of hours in a supermarket listening to mothers talk to toddlers as they shop. You will hear careful and constant instruction, reiteration, correction, and reinforcement of correct language patterns and usage. Or, if you have studied a second language, remember how much time you had to spend memorizing, listening, and practicing to become fluent.

Listening and speaking are both consciously purposive activities for which we need training to do well. The idea that some people are born listeners or born speakers is a fiction. It's a copout for people who don't want to try harder.

MISCONCEPTION NUMBER TWO: LISTENING IS PASSIVE

One of the most common misconceptions we have in our American way of life is the idea that work is always active. We seem to think that if we don't "see" something happening, work is not being done. So thinking is not often defined as work. Children are encouraged to "do something"—join the Little League, scouts, clubs. They are enrolled in camps, dancing lessons, junior business associations, and extracurricular activities. Students are encouraged to "get involved"—join the students' government, join a club or fraternity or association, contribute time to charities, and attend social events. Time spent "doing nothing" is assumed to be time wasted. In businesses and corporations people spend much of their working day going to meetings, having lunch, traveling, doing anything to look busy. Employees learn very quickly how to "look busy" when the boss comes around, even though no specific action is required at the moment. Also, scholars, whose business is thinking, have to list specific activities to their administrators to prove they really are working. In our culture, movement is equated with work.

This American orientation toward a definition of work with visible activity leads us to view listening as passive. After all, you can't see anyone listening, so they must not be "doing" anything. What we have done instead is to define the visible signs of listening as the activity itself. You will understand this statement if you think back to when you were in high school. Think about the most boring class you had in high school. You didn't want to be caught daydreaming, so what did you do? You perfected the "student's stare." You put your chin in your hand, opened your eyes real wide, and nodded periodically as though you were agreeing with what was being said. If you were clever, you remembered to throw in a frown once in a while to show you were trying to understand something particularly difficult. You smiled occasionally to show you were glad to have something so interesting to listen to in school. Meanwhile your mind went on vacation. It worked perfectly. You had learned that activity equates with work.

> When I began teaching I learned very quickly that I couldn't tell by looking who was listening and who wasn't. I had one student who always sat in the back, tilted his chair against the wall, and seemed to go to sleep. Finally one day I got fed up and challenged him. I told him that if he only meant to sleep, he could do it at home on his own time. He sat up, pushed his hat back, and recited to me the last ten minutes of my lecture. Boy, was I embarrassed.

One consequence of defining listening by its visible signs is to deny the active nature of real listening. When you are listening, your mind is extremely busy receiving and sorting out new ideas and relating them to what you already know and making new connections with old information. Real listening involves taking in new information and checking it against what you already know, selecting important ideas from unimportant ideas, searching for categories to store the information in (or creating new categories), and predicting what's coming next in order to be ready for it. The explanation of hearing and listening in the next chapter will help to make the active nature of listening clearer. When you're listening, your brain is busy actively reconstructing what the speaker is saying into meaningful units in terms of your own experience. But all this activity takes place in your brain; none of it necessarily shows itself outwardly. So it often looks like nothing is being done.

> One of the things I found most frustrating about working in a group was that no one ever seemed to be listening to me. It was like I was always talking to

myself. But then when it came time to prepare the final report, I discovered that the other group members knew a lot of the things I had been talking about. I was surprised to find out they had been listening after all. Especially John. I had thought he was a total deadhead.

MISCONCEPTION NUMBER THREE: I'M A GOOD LISTENER WHEN I TRY

Most people vastly overestimate their own listening skills. One clever educator illustrates this to people who take his workshop on listening skills by having each person introduce herself to the class. Then he asks each of them to name the person who is sitting to her left. Most people can't do it.

If you ask most people what their listening efficiency is, they will tell you that they remember about 75 to 80 percent of what they hear. Most people think they are good listeners. Research findings directly contradict this perception. The research finding most often cited to illustrate this poor listening efficiency comes from the work of Nichols (1957) who found that the average white-collar worker demonstrates only about 25 percent listening efficiency. This means that the average person only remembers about one-quarter of what he or she hears. Both these percentages are in comparison to the ideal of 100 percent recall, a feat only accomplished by fictional detectives and a few unusual persons who have perfect auditory recall (like some people have photographic memories).

The real test of listening skills is, of course, not what you can do on a listening test, but how well you understand and remember the things you have to understand and remember to get along in your daily life. When the television news broadcast is over, how much of what you heard do you remember? Can you pick out the main points when someone is giving a speech? Can you understand and remember oral instructions? How good are you at discovering people's feelings when they are talking to you? Can you distinguish between a genuinely good business deal and a scam? Can you pick out the arguments and evidence in a political speech? Can you pick out the different instruments in a band or identify the theme of a symphony? All these tasks are related to your ability to listen effectively, and skill at these tasks is important to your welfare. But most people are only partially successful at any of these tasks.

The fact is that most of us would like to think we are better listeners (more intelligent, more sensitive, more beautiful) than we really are. Listening is hard work, and we don't apply ourselves to the task unless there is a clear payoff. But unless we practice and sharpen our listening skills and develop good listening habits, it may be too late when opportunity knocks. When you're in the middle of a business deal or in the middle of a physics lecture is not the time to start practicing listening skills.

One of the hardest things about college is taking notes. It's real hard to listen and write at the same time. I find I can do one or the other. But the professor doesn't slow down for you to write. It's a real problem.

THE RHETORICAL PROCESS

Now that we have discussed some of the problems associated with learning to listen, we should address what we can do about it. In this book we will take a rhetorical approach to the listening process. That means we will analyze what we want to accomplish and then figure out how to do it. Traditionally the study of rhetoric has been applied to speaking. Speakers have been taught how to figure out what they want to accomplish and then to figure out what steps will lead them to their goals. Since listening is the counterpart to speaking, the same approach should also be effective in teaching and learning listening skills.

The *rhetorical process* seems deceptively simple and consists of four important steps. First you figure out what your goal is—what you want to accomplish. Second, you analyze the situation in which you will accomplish the goal and the needs, desires, interests, and values of the people who make up the situation. From that information you can then proceed to the third step and select appropriate behaviors that will enable you to succeed. The fourth and final step is to evaluate how successful you were, so you can improve next time. While the outline of the steps seems simple, each individual step is difficult. Unless you know what is possible and appropriate in a particular situation, it's difficult to select a goal. And how do you figure out what other people's hopes and feelings are? Finally what does it mean to select a strategy? In this book we will address all these problems in detail in later chapters.

Step 1. Choosing a Listening Goal   Speakers are taught they can choose among three possible goals: to inform, to persuade, or to entertain. While they may elect to combine these goals—to persuade by entertaining, for example—they must concentrate on a single goal to be successful. Listeners, too, must have goals if they want to be effective. As a listener you may elect to listen to understand, to listen to maintain a relationship, to listen to decide, or to listen to enjoy. In this book a chapter will be devoted to each of these purposes showing you how to accomplish the specific goal you select. There will be another chapter teaching you how to select an appropriate goal for yourself.

Let's take some simple examples to make the process clear. When you're in school, you have to spend a lot of time listening to teachers lecture. Science teachers talk about biology, chemistry, and physics. Social science teachers talk about psychology, sociology, anthropology, history, and geography. English teachers talk about writing and literature. Mathematics teachers talk about mathematics. Having to listen to all those teachers every day can be hard work, but you make it even harder if you choose an inappropriate listening goal.

Many times students don't listen well because they say the lecture (or the teacher) is boring. The choice of the word "boring" is a giveaway that those students are expecting to be entertained when they listen. They are listening to enjoy. Listening to enjoy is an appropriate goal for a concert or a play, but it's an inappropriate goal for listening to a lecture. Students at a lecture should be listening to understand. When you're listening to understand, the message is either clear or not clear, but it's never "boring." "Boring" is the opposite of "entertaining," which is an appropriate standard only when you're expecting to be entertained. You wouldn't criticize a comedian for being "confusing." Comedians are not supposed to be clear, because they are entertaining you and not teaching you. So you shouldn't criticize teachers for being "boring," because they are not expected to entertain you, only to teach.

Or, take another example. When friends or family talk together about their lives and interests, they sometimes have disagreements that can turn into real fights. Sometimes these fights are caused by a failure to select an appropriate listening goal. Let's take a sample conversation and analyze it to see how things can go wrong because someone chose the wrong listening goal:

> "Oh, Marianne, things are just awful at work. We're so behind that we'll never catch up, and the supervisor is on our case all the time. The copy machine is down, and we have to go down to another department and borrow theirs, and they're busy, too, so they don't like us there. And that supervisor! There are no words for how bad she is! Someday I'm really going to tell her off!"

> "Well, that would be a dumb thing to do. What would you do without that job? You have to pay your half of the rent, you know. I think you have a bad attitude."

> "Oh, really? *I* have a bad attitude! What about you? I suppose you're perfect! You never have a bad day, and I haven't heard you complaining about the people you work with either! Boy, you're no kind of a friend! Never catch me talking to you again!"

In this case, the speaker was expecting the listener to be listening to maintain the relationship; she was looking for sympathetic understanding. Instead, the listener chose to listen to decide; Marianne made a judgment about what the speaker was saying and decided that it was wrong. By judging the speaker's feelings to be wrong, she cut off the conversation and may possibly have damaged the relationship permanently. Listening sympathetically to maintain a relationship requires you to understand and reflect back to the speaker what you hear. You must withhold your own feelings and ideas. By misunderstanding what her listening goal should have been in that situation, Marianne made her friend even more unhappy and probably is now unhappy herself. Setting an appropriate *listening goal* is such an important topic we have devoted a whole chapter to it.

Step 2. Analyzing the Listeners and the Situation   Once you have decided what you're listening for, there is another important task before you. You must analyze the people you're listening to and analyze the situation in which you will be listening. You do this analysis for two reasons: (1) You want to know what to expect so you can be prepared and (2) you want to select specific listening behaviors appropriate for each situation. In each chapter we will direct your attention to the important factors in a situation that may affect how you listen. Here we provide a brief description of what such an analysis might look like for our two examples.

In the first instance, the lecture situation, speakers are taught to discover what their listeners' expectations are and to adapt to them. Good lecturers know that the students are expecting to be entertained as well as informed and generally include some entertaining stories in their lectures. Good listeners, on the other hand, should understand that the speaker expects them to listen for information and should adapt their behavior to that purpose. In this way both speakers and listeners adapt to one another and come to a mutual definition of what's expected in the situation.

In the second example, the conversation between two friends, each person can figure out what the other expects of him or her by using a process called *dual perspective*. Each person asks him or herself, "If I were that person, what would I expect (feel, think, believe, value)?" By understanding that the other person may have different, and equally valid, views of the world or of the particular situation, the participants can learn to understand what the other person expects of them. So Marianne can figure out how she would feel in her friend's place, and give her some sympathy. The friend (when she calms down) can figure out that Marianne is not going to want to hear the same complaints over and over and be careful not to impose on Marianne's sympathy too often. The process of friendship, like the learning situation described earlier, is a process of give-and-take, leading to a mutual agreement on what each person will do in the particular situation.

Step 3. Choosing an Appropriate Strategy   The third step in the rhetorical approach to communication—both in speaking and in listening—is the choice of behaviors appropriate to the situation, which we have called *strategies*. We say "appropriate" strategies, because there is no one right way to listen. Even in the same situation, different people may choose different strategies and still be successful. If you're successful, the strategy was appropriate; if you fail, it wasn't. Strategies are neither right nor wrong, just more or less effective. It's like catching a fish. It doesn't matter what bait you use, just as long as you catch the fish.

We have already shown how an understanding of the situation can lead the speaker and the listener to appropriate goals in the specific situation. In our lecture situation, the student decided to listen to understand and quit calling the lecture boring. He chose a strategy of listening to identify the main ideas and to see the relationship between the main ideas. After the lecturer analyzed the situation and the listeners, she decided it was only fair to make the lecture as interesting as possible and included some entertaining stories to illustrate the main points.

In our second example, Marianne chose a goal of maintaining her friendly relationship with her roommate. After she analyzed her friend's frame of mind and the situation, she decided not to tell her friend she was wrong. Instead, Marianne listened quietly without interrupting, and said she sometimes felt the same way. Then she changed the subject to something more positive. If she was really worried about her friend's situation, she could choose a different time (when her friend wasn't so upset) to discuss the situation seriously.

In each case the person chose a course of action that might lead to the achievement of the goals of both people in the situation. The student had to take the instructor's goals into account, and Marianne had to be aware of what her roommate needed. Even so, we have to warn you, there is no guarantee that you will be successful. Even if you have chosen an appropriate goal, studied the situation, and carefully planned your behavior, sometimes things out of your control can cause you to fail. But your chances of succeeding are much improved if you know what you're trying to accomplish and how to go about it.

Step 4. Evaluating Your Own Performance The final step in the rhetorical process is to evaluate your own performance so you can improve in the future. We call communication a process to emphasize the idea that it never actually "begins" at any particular point and never actually "ends" at a given time. Communication is always evolving. When the student in our first example attends a lecture, the communication associated with the lecture doesn't just include the actual time spent in the class. While there is a specified time set aside for the formal "lecture," even before that time both instructor and students are thinking about and planning what will happen. Then after class both instructor and students (hopefully) are still thinking about the ideas and talking with other people about them. The formal lecture is just one part of a larger relationship between students and lecturer that includes questions and answers, exams, papers, and casual conversations. Sometimes students remember and apply what they learned in the classroom months or years later, suddenly feeling, "So that's what it was all about! Now I understand."

> My students all do a self-evaluation after each speech, and that self-evaluation includes this question: "Knowing what you know now, what would you do different next time?" Occasionally after the last speech of the semester, students write, "Nothing. That's the last time I'll ever give a speech." How wrong they are. Sometime they'll have to speak at the school board meeting or make a recommendation to their boss or ask the vice president at the bank for a loan. Those are all speeches just like the ones they gave in class. Only they don't just get a grade on those speeches. Success or failure is more serious when they're speaking in the real world.

The student in the first example may find out how successful he was when he receives his test scores. At least he will learn from those scores whether he's listening for what the instructor thinks are the most important points. Or the student may decide that he has mastered the lecture material when he can explain it to someone else clearly. It would be an inappropriate measure of success to say he liked or didn't like the course. Liking or not liking the course is related to how entertaining it is, not to whether or not the material was mastered. Since we have established that the student's goal should be to understand the material, our measure for success should be related to that goal.

Similarly, if the instructor's goal is to give information, it's not appropriate to judge success by how much the students liked the course. It's more appropriate to judge success by their scores on the exam or by their performance on a paper or completion of a project. If the students could demonstrate their understanding on an exam, the instructor could consider her or himself successful.

It's a little more difficult to evaluate how successful you are in personal relationships. Marianne will have to decide how she will know whether she is successful by specifying what she thinks friendship means. She might decide that she wants her roommate to listen to her problems without interrupting her and without telling her she's right or wrong. How you define and measure friendship depends partly on what you learn by watching what other people do and what you personally want or need from a relationship. But if you don't specify what friendship means to you, you run the risk of never being satisfied. That's why evaluating your own performance is so important; you have to set criteria by which you would know if you were successful.

After you have evaluated your own performance, you go back to the first step again. You decide what your goals in the next situation are and then you analyze that situation. Every situation you find yourself in is a little different from the last, so you have to change your goals and strategies to fit the situation. That's what we mean by being rhetorical. Being rhetorical involves considering the context and the relationship in the situations you find yourself in and adapting your own behavior.

SUMMARY

In this chapter we described three common misconceptions about listening: (1) that listening is natural, (2) that listening is passive, and (3) that you can listen well when you try. We also defined a four-step rhetorical process by which you can learn to become a better listener. The four steps were (1) set yourself an appropriate goal, (2) analyze the situation and the speaker, (3) select an appropriate listening strategy, and (4) evaluate your own performance as a listener.

In the next chapter we will detail how the psychological process of listening differs from the physical process of hearing. We hope to convince you that listening is not a natural or a simple process but a consciously learned behavior that you have to understand and practice to get good at. Armed with this understanding, you will be ready to learn to set appropriate listening goals and improve your performance in listening.

SUGGESTED ACTIVITIES

1. Collect articles, cartoons, songs, or commercials that relate to ineffective listening. Analyze what problems are illustrated by each of these examples. Can you find commonalities that indicate categories of problems?

2. Contact counselors in local elementary schools, high schools, and universities and ask whether they teach listening skills in the classroom. Contact managers or supervisors in local companies or businesses and ask whether they provide training in listening for their employees. If they do, ask about their programs. If they don't, find out whether they think listening is an important skill and whether they think it can be taught and learned.

3. Interview a supervisor in a local company or business and ask about the importance of listening skills in their occupation. Ask what their major problems are and what advice they could give you about listening effectively.

4. Interview professionals—attorneys, doctors, psychologists—and ask about the importance of listening in their occupations. Ask what their major problems are and how they learned to listen. Ask what advice they would give you about learning to listen effectively.

REFERENCES AND RECOMMENDED READING

Barbara, Dominick A. *How to Make People Listen to You.* Springfield, IL: Charles C. Thomas, 1971.

Barker, Larry L. *Listening Behavior.* Englewood Cliffs, NJ: Prentice-Hall, 1971.

Hirsh, Robert O. *Listening: A Way to Process Information Aurally,* Dubuque, IA: Corsuch Scarisbrich, 1979.

Nichols, Ralph G., "Factors in Listening Comprehension." *Speech Monographs* 15 (1948): 154–163.

Nichols, Ralph G., and Leonard A Stevens. *Are You Listening?* New York: McGraw-Hill, 1957, pp. 12–13.

Phillips, Gerald M., and Julia T. Wood. *Communication and Human Relations.* New York: Macmillan, 1983.

Steil, Lyman, Larry L. Barker, and Kittie W. Watson. *Effective Listening.* Reading, MA: Addison-Wesley, 1983.

Wolff, Florence I., Nadine C. Marsnik, William S. Tracy, and Ralph G. Nichols. *Perceptive Listening.* New York: Holt, Rinehart and Winston, 1983.

chapter 2

What Listening Is—Physical and Psychological Process

When you finish this chapter you should be able to:

1. Distinguish between the processes of hearing and listening.
2. Describe the physical process of hearing.
3. Name and describe the five components of the hearing process.
4. Describe the psychological process of listening.
5. Describe how sounds are turned into information in the brain.
6. Explain the statement that there is no necessary or direct relationship between the words a speaker says and what a listener understands.
7. Explain the relative importance of acoustic cues and listener expectations to the ability to understand what we hear.
8. Describe the relationship between good listening skills and success in a career.
9. Identify and describe physical, social, and psychological factors that can interfere with listening.

When you have finished this chapter you should be able to define these important concepts:

1. hearing
2. listening
3. outer ear, middle ear, inner ear
4. malleus, incus, stapes
5. oval window
6. cochlea

7. frequency and intensity
8. loudness and pitch
9. information
10. acoustic cues
11. physical and physiological factors
12. social factors
13. psychological factors

None of us is perfect at listening. The complexities of our language system and of our daily experiences ensure that we often make mistakes that end in misunderstandings, arguments, and problems. A lot of those misunderstandings seem silly or stupid after we have worked them out, but they were certainly real at the time. In Chapter 1 we described some typical problems that arise from ineffective or inappropriate listening practices. In this chapter we consider the processes of hearing and listening in an effort to point out where problems may lie.

Hearing and listening are deceptively simple operations. After all, we have been hearing and listening all our lives. Like the centipede who couldn't walk when he asked himself which foot came first, few of us have ever questioned exactly how we listen and understand. Luckily for us, it isn't necessary to understand how we listen to be able to do it. But an understanding of the processes of hearing and listening will help us to be more effective listeners. We will have a better idea of what can go wrong and what measures we can take to prevent or correct mistakes.

The first step in understanding the processes of hearing and listening is to understand that they are in fact two separate processes. *Hearing* is a physiological process by which we perceive changes in air pressure and turn them into electrochemical processes in the brain. Hearing is an automatic process that goes on constantly without our conscious control. *Listening,* on the other hand, is a conscious learned behavior of selectively responding to the sounds we hear. Listening is a psychological process of identifying, classifying, and interpreting electrochemical processes into meaning and action.

To illustrate the physical process of hearing, we describe how sounds are received and processed. There are basically five physiological components in the hearing process: outer ear, middle ear, inner ear, auditory nerve, and brain. The outer and middle ears serve to transmit the mechanical energy of sound waves to the inner ear, which transforms that mechanical energy into electrochemical energy. The electrochemical impulses created in the inner ear are then transmitted through the auditory nerve to brain centers that interpret the signals into meaning. The psychological process of interpretation of sounds by the brain constitutes listening. We consider each process separately.

HEARING: THE PHYSICAL PROCESS

Hearing is what the ear does. The ear collects, amplifies, and transmits the movements of the sound waves outside the ear to the inner ear where these movements are converted into nerve impulses. Sounds exist as minute changes of air pressure. All changes in air pressure affect the eardrum, which is a membrane stretched across the opening in the skull that forms the ear. Large or intense changes in air pressure are felt as pain, such as when you go up or down quickly in an elevator or airplane or when you hear a very loud noise nearby. Very tiny changes in air pressure aren't registered on the eardrum. But within a range of between 20 and 20,000 cycles per second most people "hear" changes in air pressure. It's important to remember that here is no difference to the ear between the changes in air pressure caused by a bird singing, an automobile passing, a typewriter clattering, or a human voice speaking. All changes in air pressure are registered in the same way by the eardrum.

Outer and Middle Ear—Mechanical Energy

The part of the ear outside the head and up to the eardrum is called the *outer ear.* The function of the outer ear is to capture changes in air pressure and funnel them into the ear. The next part of the ear, called the *middle ear,* is a small passage inside the skull that amplifies the signals from the eardrum and passes them on to the *inner ear.* Inside the middle ear there are three small bones called the *malleus,* the *incus,* and the *stapes.* These three small bones are attached to each other and are suspended inside the middle ear by ligaments attaching them to the skull. These bones work somewhat like the jointed arm of a puppet; movements in one bone are transmitted to the next and then to the third bone. The malleus is attached to the eardrum and it vibrates with the vibrations of the eardrum. Those vibrations are transmitted to the incus and then to the stapes, which is connected to the inner ear.

The middle ear performs two important functions: (1) It amplifies the vibrations received by the eardrum and (2) it protects the sensitive inner ear from damage by loud noises. The small bones of the middle ear act like levers to increase the acoustic energy from the eardrum to the inner ear by a factor of about

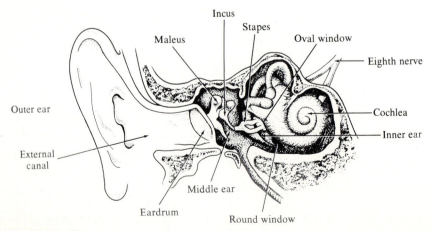

Figure 2.1   The ear.

1.5. This function helps us to hear noises that we might not otherwise be able to detect and to distinguish between noises that are close in frequency to one another.

To protect the inner ear from damage, there is a mechanism in the middle ear that pulls these three small bones temporarily out of alignment when the eardrum registers extremely loud noises. You know this from experience if you have ever heard a loud noise like a gunshot up close. For a few seconds after the loud noise, you can't hear very clearly, because the small bones in your middle ear have been pulled out of alignment. Without this protection in the middle ear, the sensitive inner ear mechanism might be ruptured and permanently damaged by a sudden loud noise.

Inner Ear—Electrochemical Energy

It's important to remember that both the outer and the middle ears transmit sound in the form of mechanical energy. The eardrum and the bones in the middle ear vibrate to carry the sound wave from outside the head to the inner ear. The inner ear is an extremely complex organ that transforms this mechanical energy into electrochemical nerve impulses that are carried to the brain and processed into sensations of sound.

The innermost bone in the middle ear, the stapes, is connected to a membrane called the *oval window* which transmits the vibrations from the middle ear to a fluid-filled organ called the *cochlea.* The cochlea is coiled rather like a snail's shell, and the fluid inside the cochlea vibrates when it's stimulated by vibrations of the oval window. Vibrations inside the fluid of the cochlea are transmitted to the auditory nerve through thousands of small hair cells located along a membrane within the cochlea. The process of conversion from mechanical energy (vibrations of the fluid in the cochlea) to electrochemical energy (received by the auditory nerve) is very complex. Fortunately for our purposes it's enough to know that the inner ear processes the vibrations received from the middle ear and turns them into nerve impulses that are transmitted to the brain and processed there. At this point, before the nerve impulses reach the brain, there is no difference in quality between sounds; the ear does not distinguish among the sound of a jackhammer pounding, a rock band playing, or a committee deliberating.

Hearing is a continuous process that's not under our conscious control. We hear whatever there is to hear 24 hours a day. We cannot shut our ears as we can shut our eyes and shut out perception. Even when we are asleep we hear everything that goes on around us. Our brains, however, have the capacity to pay attention or not pay attention to what we hear. When we are asleep, our brains monitor what's going on outside and decide which noises to respond to or not respond to. This monitoring process also goes on when we are awake, so we select what we pay attention to and what we don't pay attention to. This selection process is the interpretation of sound that we call listening.

When I first got to college, it was awful. I was in a dorm room with two other girls, and someone was making noise 24 hours a day. If it wasn't a party, it was music, or people talking, or something else. But after a couple of weeks I got used to the noise. Now you couldn't wake me up with a fire alarm!

LISTENING: THE PSYCHOLOGICAL PROCESS

Listening can be distinguished from hearing because listening is a conscious process that takes place in the brain. Listening is something we do because we want to. When we listen we take account of some of the things we are hearing and ignore other things. We choose which sounds or aspects of sound to pay attention to depending on our purposes at the time. For example, we can listen to music just to enjoy the sounds or listen to music to identify the particular artist or group or listen to music to understand the meaning of the composer or listen to music to evaluate the expertise of the artist or group. Usually we can't do all these things at the same time. We can listen to a voice on the telephone to identify who's speaking, to understand the words, or to identify what the speaker is feeling. Often we can do all three at the same time.

Listening Is Conscious Work

You can prove to yourself that listening is conscious work by reflecting on your own experience as a listener. When you're listening to something that's very interesting, you block out all other noises. If you're concentrating hard, you may not even hear someone call your name. Or you can train yourself not to hear something that you don't want to hear. If you have to work in a noisy place, you can learn not to be disturbed by the noises around you.

> My brother was always a book worm. He never paid any attention to us when he was reading. We all thought maybe he was hard of hearing. But when he went to college, he had a hearing test. His hearing was perfect! "Oh, he hears all right," the doctor said, "he's just not listening."

For purposes of this book we can define listening as a conscious psychological process of selecting and interpreting *acoustic cues* to produce information as the basis for action. To explain that statement we need to understand more about how we select and process information in our brains. All living systems process information. Even without brains plants respond to light and moisture and heat and touch. Humans are considerably more complex than plants and in order to live, they have to process much more complex information.

Paying Attention

We said earlier that the ear doesn't distinguish between the quality of sounds. The sounds that reach the ear—from the traffic passing, the telephone ringing, the radio playing, the refrigerator humming—are all processed in exactly the same way by the ear. The brain, on the other hand, sorts out these sounds into meaningful and nonmeaningful sounds. For example, imagine you were in a room where all these sounds were going on. You would probably pay attention to the sound of the telephone above all, because you have been trained to listen for that sound. When the phone rings, you have to answer it.

Let's say that the telephone call was from some friends you had not seen in a long time, telling you they were dropping by soon to see you. The sounds of the traffic that you had not even heard before might suddenly become significant. You would probably find yourself listening for the sound of your friends' car coming up to your house and stopping. In the meantime, one of your favorite songs comes on the radio. Immediately you start to listen to the radio, although you couldn't say what was playing just before your song came on. If you really got into the song, you might even forget to listen for the sound of your friends' car and be surprised by the sound of the doorbell! You probably wouldn't hear the refrigerator running at all unless, for example, you had turned the radio off so that the room was quiet. Then you might notice when the refrigerator motor shut off, but you probably wouldn't notice when it turned on. We become so accustomed to background noises that we often don't even hear them.

Measuring Sound

Scientists have developed two different kinds of measurements for sounds—one measurement for the physical movement of air and another for the psychological interpretation of sound. Two physical properties of sound, *frequency* and *intensity,* are inherent in the sound wave itself and are measured by mechanical instruments. But when sound is interpreted we hear the psychological properties of sounds called *pitch* and *loudness.*

To understand the differences between these two measures of sound, think of the experience of having a hearing test. Hearing tests attempt to correlate these two measures of sound. The audiologist or technician who administers the test plays a tape of sounds whose intensity and frequency are known and controlled. This technician is attempting to find out at which particular frequency and intensity you begin to experience pitch and loudness. The opposite example is also instructive. Imagine a musical technician who's mixing a tape; this technician uses the subjective experiences of loudness and pitch to guide and control the intensity and frequency of the sounds being mixed. Frequency and intensity are physical characteristics of sound waves; pitch and loudness are psychological characteristics of the subjective experience of sound.

Processing Information

All the sounds that you hear are interpreted into information about what's going on in the world around you so you can respond appropriately. We tend to think of information as being contained in books or pictures or even as being stored in our brains. Unfortunately the way we talk about information reinforces this impression. We talk about sharing, storing, using, giving out, or getting information. We even talk about finding information as though it were some kind of artifact, maybe a prize or a treasure. But information, someone once noted, is the only "thing" that can be taken without being stolen. Information in books or pictures doesn't exist unless someone reads it or looks at it and understands it.

Information is not a thing; *information* exists in the orderly arrangement of parts that form a code or system that has meaning for whoever uses it. This system of parts always exists in relation to some perception of usefulness by whoever uses it. As a child, you may have had to learn the Morse Code of dots and dashes that make up the signals once used on telegraphs. You know that's a code because it's called a code. Computers also use code; they have their own languages, like BASIC, PASCAL, and FORTRAN. Sign language is a nonverbal code, and there are all kinds of secret codes that you can use to communicate only to people who know the code. But you may not have considered that the English language is also a code.

The information system most of us use when we listen to other people is the English language. English, like all languages, is a shared code system that operates according to a set of rules for its use. We learn these rules very early in life, in our second year. There are rules for the formation of meaningful sounds into words and rules for the formation of words into meaningful sentences. Very young children practice making all kinds of sounds; linguists tell us they start out making all the possible sounds in all the possible languages in the world. But they quickly stop making the sounds they don't hear in the language spoken around them. By the time most of you were six or seven, you probably couldn't make the glottal sounds used in German, and you surely couldn't make the "click" sounds used in many African languages. You had learned to make the sounds that had meaning in English, including the sound that's so difficult for many nonnative speakers, the "th" sound.

Listening Purposely

Since listening is the primary way we learn, at least when we are young, listening is a critical survival skill. In order to be able to get what we want, we have to be able to communicate with the people around us. That means using the shared language system, and that means listening purposely. We select some aspects of the sounds we are hearing to attend to and we ignore other aspects. There is some evidence that humans are particularly sensitive to the sounds of human speech. Studies of infants as young as 1 month show they are more responsive to speech sounds than to other kinds of sounds (Young, 1978). In any case, listening is an active process of construction or reconstruction of meaning that's carried out purposely. We don't just listen; we listen *for* something. We listen to make sense out of the world and to help us figure out what to do about it.

If the code is garbled (a bad connection) or unfamiliar (a foreign language), we may find ourselves unable to decode the message, and unable to interpret what we hear. What's more frustrating than trying to enjoy a movie when someone behind you keeps talking and disturbing your concentration! Or, have you ever tried to get directions from someone who didn't speak English? Hearing isn't the problem; listening is. Listening is a selective, voluntary, conscious action.

I remember my chemistry lab. It was taught by a Chinese graduate assistant. That guy was a real nice guy, but he had such a strange accent that I never did understand what he was talking about. If you didn't get it from the book, man, you didn't get it at all. That course was a real killer.

When you consider it, your brain does an incredible job of sorting out and recognizing the cues that are important to your safety and happiness. To understand this complexity, think for a moment about all the things you can tell when you listen to someone's voice over the telephone. You can recognize the identity of your friends, you can tell what kind of a mood they are in, you can tell whether they are well or ill. Even if you didn't understand the words (Jerry's a real card; he's speaking Yiddish again!), you can tell whether the sounds represent a statement or a question. Probably you can tell whether the speaker is serious or joking. All without understanding a single word. There's another whole process going on in your brain that enables you to recognize the sounds on the telephone as language and to decode and decipher the meaning of the words being spoken. Your brain carries on all these processes without your ever having to think about it.

Since listening is a consciously learned and purposeful task, we should be able to discover ways to become more effective at it. In this book we will take a rhetorical approach to listening and analyze the various components of the process to discover how to improve our performance. Chapter 3 will deal with setting listening goals, and the following chapters will illustrate how to be more effective at each of the goals you set for yourself.

PROBLEMS AND INTERFERENCES WITH THE LISTENING PROCESS

Listening is so natural to us that we seldom even think about it. When we do think about it we might say that when we listen we hear words and sentences. In fact, we don't. We "hear" sounds (varying frequencies of vibrations in the air) and our brains process these sensations into phonemes (smallest recognizable units of sound) and rhythm and intonation patterns which our brains then reconstruct into words and sentences of the spoken language. We don't hear what's said directly, we reconstruct it. And what we reconstruct is based primarily on what we expect to hear, based on our past experience of the speaker, the situation, and the language.

There is no necessary or direct relationship between the words a speaker say *and the words a listener understands.* You probably learned this lesson in schoc or at Scouts where you played some variant of a game called "Gossip." Or person in the group whispered something to her neighbor, who whispered wh he had heard to his neighbor, and so on until the last person repeated aloud wh she or he had heard. It was never the same as what the first person whispere Sometimes the difference was quite funny. Understanding what the speaker sa depends on our ability to process and interpret accurately a wide variety

different cues in the environment, including not only the sounds we hear with our ears but a lot of visual cues and all our past experience at listening.

Listening Involves Interpretation

Listening, therefore, isn't just a matter of receiving and processing sounds. It's neither instinctive nor automatic. Listening involves interpretation of the nerve impulses our brains receive from the vibrations that reach our ears. Denes and Pinson (1973) tell us that we don't recognize words from the acoustic or sound cues; we recognize them from the context and because we know the patterns of what's possible in the situation. In other words, we predict what's possible to be said and then we prepare ourselves to hear that. For example, if someone in France said, "Pas de la Rhone que nous," an English speaker who didn't know French would hear, "Paddle your own canoe." It depends on what we expect to hear. You can probably think of other examples of sentences that are easy to misunderstand in the wrong context.

> When I was on vacation the funniest thing happened to me. We were camping down in South Carolina. Well, one night I just couldn't sleep for anything, so I went to the local camp store and asked the guy there for some sleeping pills, you know, Sominex. The guy gave me fish bait! He thought I has asked for "salmon eggs." We had a heck of a time getting it straight.

Listening Involves Prediction

We understand speech by combining our knowledge of the sounds we hear with our knowledge of what's possible given the rules of the language, the subject matter under discussion, and the circumstances or situation in which the speaking takes place. If we didn't use all these cues, we would find it impossible to understand people from different parts of the world. Just imagine a conversation among someone from Mississippi, someone from Maine, someone from India, and someone from Australia, and you will readily understand that we use more than acoustic cues to understand speech. Although all the people from these different places are speaking English, the sounds they produce vary widely. We must use cues other than just sounds to interpret what the speakers are saying.

Usually we have many more cues than we need to understand speech, so we can often predict what will be said even before we hear the words. Fry (1977) tells us that when we listen on an ordinary telephone, we hear something less than half the range of frequencies we receive when we talk with someone in the same room. Yet we don't have any difficulty understanding other people on the phone, because we have a good idea what we can expect to hear.

INTERFERENCES WITH LISTENING

There are, however, a number of factors that can interfere with our ability to listen well. Some of these factors are external noises, some are social, arising

from the situations we find ourselves in, and some are psychological or internal to our own behavior. In the next section we consider some of the interferences with listening to help us understand how we can go wrong and how we can correct or compensate for possible failures.

Interference Number One
Our Culture Emphasizes Speaking Over Listening.

Most people seem to consider speaking a more important activity than listening, maybe because speaking seems more active. Most communication courses focus on speaking; there are very few courses devoted exclusively to listening. We get assertiveness training, not training in being passive. We have courses devoted to helping people become less shy, but no courses designed to help people become less overbearing and domineering. Quiet people are sometimes pictured as victims—those people who cannot control their own lives. As we said before, we seem to confuse activity with action and assume that the person who's quietly listening isn't doing anything very important. The mistaken belief that people who are listening are passive and let others control their lives leads us to value the listening less than speaking. While the study of speaking is more than 2000 years old, there is no corresponding systematic study of listening.

Many people also seem to think that the person who knows how to talk well is the most popular person, the "life of the party." We call the quiet people at social occasions "wallflowers" and feel sorry for them. Students often report that they admire their friends who can talk to all kinds of people and list that ability as one of the criteria for having good communication skills. Many students seem to feel that skill at conversation is something some people are born with (although they themselves apparently were not).

It's also the person who's most verbal, or sometimes only most vocal, who often seems to win the argument. How many times have you lost an argument to someone who could talk faster or better or longer than you could? Were you really convinced that person was right, or did you just give up talking? And if you just gave up talking, was it because the other person wasn't really listening to what you were saying? In that case who really won the argument? Still, most people would tend to say that the person who has the last word won the argument. So the person who can speak well is often looked on as smarter than the person who remains quiet.

Listening and Leadership   We also think of people who talk well as leaders; we seldom credit leaders with the ability to listen. On television we see leaders giving speeches; in the newspapers they are quoted at length. Candidates debate, harangue, persuade, plead. Leaders direct, delegate, prescribe, command. One of the most persistent and difficult problems in organizations is that information gets quickly from the top levels down to the bottom, but it's very difficult for workers to get a supervisor or manager to listen to them. People who become leaders seem to assume that it's their business to talk and everyone else's business to listen. The explosion of the space shuttle *Challenger* may be a tragic example of managers who didn't listen.

What's not obvious in the newspapers or in television or radio accounts is that leaders would not be leaders long if they didn't listen to the people who are supporting them and help those followers achieve their goals. Real leaders must be quintessential listeners. They must understand what their supporters want and what's possible for them to achieve. Leaders who stop listening to pursue their own goals eventually lose their power to lead; sooner or later they are replaced by other leaders who are listening more carefully to what the people want. Leaders have to be able to speak well, but what they say has to be based on what they learned by listening well. Dictators, like Marcos in the Philippines, lose their power to lead when they stop listening to what the people want and pursue their own individual goals.

> We elected Bill president of our fraternity last year because he was such a personable guy and he talked so well. We thought he'd make a great president. But it turned out that he doesn't listen to how we want the fraternity run. He thinks because we elected him president, he can do things his way. Well, he's going to find out next year. You can bet he won't get another office in our organization!

Listening and Popularity   The same statement is true of people who are labeled as smart or popular. Popular people have to be good listeners, too. The "life of the party" may have an interesting line of patter and jokes, but those jokes are carefully selected and rehearsed to be appropriate for the people who are listening (Zolten, 1982). Good conversationalists are no more born than are good teachers. Both kinds of people have spent a long time listening to the people they deal with and learning how best to talk to them. In other words, the people who are able to talk to different kinds of people learned that skill by listening carefully to different kinds of people and learning what those folks were interested in. People who only talk about their own concerns are seldom looked on as interesting or smart: They are considered dreadful bores. We like people who are interested in the same things we are interested in. If you want to become popular or be looked on as smart, the best way to begin is to learn how to listen well to figure out what other people are interested in. Then you can begin to work on speaking skills. But if you start out with the speaking skills, you will have built the house without the foundation.

Listening Professionally   Really good listeners can often command money and prestige in our society. These people are the psychiatrists, lawyers, salespeople, and corporate executives who listen for a living. Psychologists and psychiatrists are paid high fees to help clients understand and solve their own problems by listening to the clients talk about their lives. Good lawyers, too, base their advice on a detailed knowledge of their clients' individual situations and on what remedies and resources are available to their clients in such situations. Without good listening skills, these professionals would never be able to learn enough about their clients to serve them well.

Salespeople might appear to be primarily talkers. After all, they have to talk to sell the product. But you know from your own experience that if the salesperson doesn't direct attention to your own concerns, you will not buy. If you're interested in the best computer, the salesperson who talks about the cheapest will not sell to you. If you're concerned about the safety of a power tool, the salesperson had better not spend time talking about all the fancy applications. To be successful, salespeople have to know all about their products, but they also have to know all about their customers. Salespeople need to know what customers want, what their interests and values are, and just what kinds of arguments will appeal to them. How do they find out about their customers? By listening. Writing about the importance of effective listening in business, Montgomery (1981) noted, "It's a well-known fact that in most companies about 20 percent of the salespeople sell around 80 percent of the company's products or services each year. The main difference between salespeople in most instances is that the successful salespeople are good listeners." Good salespeople maintain good relationships with their customers, because repeat business is important to them.

Corporate executives must command a vast knowledge of their own organizations and of the larger business world in which they work. Most of the information they need to do their jobs well is never written down anywhere; executives get their information by listening carefully to the right people. Learning whom to listen to and what to listen for are important skills, and they are skills that can be taught and learned. My grandmother used to say, "You never learn anything with your mouth open." Good listening skills are the basis for success in some of the most highly paid professions, as well as the basis for popularity.

So we see that the idea that talking is more important than listening is based on a fallacy, or a false idea. In fact, the most successful speakers are the most effective listeners. Instead of being a one-way process from speaker to listener, communication is a relationship that involves both listening and responding. But the idea that speaking well is the most important element of popularity or success may lead many people to neglect the listening element of communication skills. It's one factor that interferes with the development of good listening skills.

Interference Number Two
Physical and Physiological Conditions
Can Interfere With Listening.

The physical situations we find ourselves in will affect our ability to listen effectively. "The mind can absorb what the seat of the pants can endure," is one way of saying that physical comfort is very important to how well we can listen. Both outside distraction and inside discomfort—physical and physiological factors— can limit attention and reduce listening effectiveness.

Physical Distractions   Outside distractions that interfere with listening can be anything from the person next to you tapping a pencil to the lack of light to see the speaker clearly. If you're trying to listen, other sounds in the environment can either mask the sounds you're trying to hear or can compete for your attention. Maybe you're trying to listen to a speaker and someone behind you is whispering. In a restaurant the background music or the noise from the kitchen or other diners' conversations are sometimes so loud you can't listen effectively. Parties and ball games are notorious for being poor environments for listening, because the many competing conversations reach such a high level of noise that people find themselves shouting to be heard. To some extent you can overcome distractions caused by other sounds by concentrating hard, but sometimes it's best to move or to find another environment in which to continue what you were trying to do.

Distractions aren't necessarily other sounds in the environment. Listening is difficult when there are visual distractions, too. In a public place where people are coming and going, it's often difficult to keep your mind on one thing. Your eyes are naturally drawn to movements, and your mind seems to follow your eyes away from what you were listening to. The television is a great source of distraction, even if the sound is turned down. You may find yourself watching the images chase one another across the screen and discover you haven't heard anything your friend has said for several minutes. And it's almost impossible to hold a serious conversation while driving, because your attention is constantly distracted by the other vehicles or by the passing scenery. Even smells (especially unpleasant ones) can affect your attention and keep you from listening carefully.

Professional listeners like psychologists and salespeople pay careful attention to the physical comfort of their clients. Someone who's sitting on a hard chair or a chair that's too large or too small cannot pay careful attention to what's going on around them. Other physical discomforts like smoke in the room, lights that are inadequate or too bright, or a room that's too hot or too cold can effectively prevent clients from paying attention. When you're uncomfortable all you can think about is getting out of there. Listening depends to a great degree on the physical comfort of the listener.

> It was an awful interview. After we introduced ourselves and shook hands, he said to sit down anywhere. There were only two sorts of couches, so I sat down on the nearest one. There were no arms and when you sat back you were practically lying down. So I had to sit hunched forward resting my arms on my knees. The interview lasted half an hour, and when I tried to stand up I practically fell down. I had a cramp in my leg and my neck was getting stiff. I can't remember anything that was said in that interview.

Physiological Distractions Physiological conditions like pain and hunger can also affect a person's attention and prevent him or her from listening carefully. It's hard to listen when you haven't had breakfast or dinner; images of food keep getting between you and what the speaker is saying. Or, if you have a headache or a cramp in your leg, the pain keeps distracting you from other ideas. Fatigue is another source of distraction that can interfere with attention even when you know it's important to listen carefully. Have you ever tried to take a test when you're tired? When you're very tired your mind seems to drift in and out, and you can't pay attention or remember as well as you can when you're fresh.

Controlling Distractions   To the extent that you have any control over the environment in which you must listen, you can alleviate the problems caused by distractions. You can avoid distractions like noise, smoke, bad light, and uncomfortable furniture, or you can do your best to improve the conditions under which you must work. By improving the situation in which listening takes place, you can improve listening performance. If you're responsible for the situation in which other people must listen, you can greatly increase their listening performance by ensuring that they have comfortable conditions for doing their work. If you're leading a meeting or teaching a class, you can make sure distractions are kept to a minimum and that everyone is comfortable and can see the speaker well. Sometimes these simple preventive measures will increase your effectiveness far out of proportion to the effort it took.

Sometimes you can also prevent or alleviate physiological discomfort that may interfere with your own ability to listen. Make sure you don't go to a lecture or an interview when you're tired or hungry. Choose a seat or a position in which you're comfortable (but not too comfortable). If you're in charge of a situation in which other people will be listening to you, it would be a good idea to consider your listeners' comfort. If changing the temperature of the room or the level of the light will improve listening performance, the results of thoughtfulness about listeners' comfort will pay off for everyone concerned.

Interference Number Three
Social Factors Can Prevent Effective Listening.

Physical factors in the environment aren't the only factors that work to prevent effective listening. There are also social factors that can interfere with listening. By *social factors* we mean those elements of the situation that have to do with the interaction of the people who are present together. In most social situations there are established patterns of behavior that may promote or inhibit effective listening, and there may also be distractions or interferences from the attitudes or behaviors of any of the people in the situation. It would take a whole book to deal comprehensively with this topic, so a few examples must serve to illustrate the social factors that may affect listening behavior.

Social Distractions   One social factor that may interfere with effective listening is in the form of distractions. We are all familiar with the experience of trying to listen to more than one thing at a time. At a high school reunion, a ball game, or a party, you may find yourself talking to one person but constantly looking around to see who else is there and what else is going on. If the radio or the television is on, you may tune in to that instead of listening to the person you're with. Alternatively, if you're trying to pay attention to the television, people coming in and out may distract you. Listening to other people's conversations is another temptation to distraction. Whenever more than two people are present, the temptation to pay attention to someone other than the person you're with is always there.

When you're trying to listen to more than one thing at a time, you tend to "tune in" and "tune out" alternately and not comprehend anything completely.

You may find yourself nodding or saying "Uh-huh" to encourage the idea that you're really listening, while in fact you're paying attention to something else entirely. You probably mastered this art in high school classes that bored you. You will also notice that the parents of small children exhibit this behavior. Very few people are genuinely capable of paying attention to more than one thing at a time, so social distractions often interfere with effective listening.

Social Rules There are also social occasions at which you're not expected to listen. For example, high school commencement speeches and announcements on the public address system in grocery stores are probably times when you don't pay strict attention. You can probably compile a long list of occasions at which you aren't really expected to listen carefully. Reception lines at formal occasions are notoriously those times when no one listens to anyone else, as one woman proved to her own satisfaction. As she proceeded from one dignitary to the next in the line, she murmured to each, "My mother just died." "So delighted," was the usual response.

One important unwritten rule of group behavior is that the people who have been members of a group for a long time are expected to speak and newcomers are expected to listen. This rule is most obvious when it's broken. The newcomer who spends too much time speaking in a group may be labeled "pushy" or "gabby" or "impolite." Older members, on the other hand, may not feel they have much to learn from newer members, and they will not spend much time listening. The study of who listens to whom in a group is a fascinating one.

Status in the group is another social factor that may affect listening behavior. We generally expect people with lower status to listen to people with higher status. We don't expect people of high social status to spend time listening to their inferiors. Professors talk and students listen; executives direct and subordinates carry out; officers command and soldiers obey. So people who find themselves in a room with people whom they define as their "social superiors" are constrained to listen (or pretend to), while those "social superiors" are obligated to speak. This isn't, of course, a hard and fast rule; who speaks and who listens (and what they speak about) will depend on a combination of social rules that affects the definition of appropriate behavior in any situation. The only executive at a meeting of secretaries may well feel it more appropriate to listen than to speak. But, in general, people who hold high status in a group find their behavior, even their listening behavior, constrained by the expectations of the other people in the group.

There are other unwritten rules of behavior in groups that affect who speaks and who listens, and many rules will be specific to specific groups. The important point about the effect of social constraints on listening behavior is that *we are usually not consciously aware of the existence or effect of the rules we follow in groups.* We may find ourselves thrust into roles or behaving in ways that aren't the most effective for us or for the group because we are behaving in ways that are "expected" of us. It's entirely possible that a newcomer to the group may have something very important or interesting to contribute if anyone was listening. Executives or supervisors who listen to employees' comments may learn something important about the organization, if they are willing to listen. Parents who listen to their children may find that the children will return the courtesy. We have to be aware of our own listening behavior to analyze its effectiveness instead of being bound by the rules of particular social occasions.

Social Expectations   What are closely related to the rules for proper behavior in groups are the kinds of social expectations that we learn in regard to certain kinds of people. In some cultures, for instance, old people are highly respected and what they say carries great weight in the community. In our own culture the emphasis is on youth. "Things are different now than when you were young," is a common sentiment, and there is much less emphasis on listening to old people. Recently, there has been a strong tendency to listen carefully to anything that celebrities say, whether or not those celebrities have any expertise in the topic on which they are quoted. Movie and television stars advertise commercial products or run for political office. They raise enormous amounts of money for charitable causes, all on the basis of their fame as entertainers. "I'm not a doctor," says one such star, "but I play a doctor on television. And I take Brand X for headaches." Too many people seem to think being famous is reason enough to listen to anything a person says.

A final and very dangerous social constraint on whom we listen to is that of similarity and difference. In order to deal with the complexity of our lives, we tend to stereotype people and deal with them as types of a larger group. So Polish or Irish or Catholics or Jews get lumped together into categories, and we assume that they all resemble one another in important ways. But we often find it very hard to listen to people who aren't like us. Differences in skin color or ethnic background or exotic accent often affect our listening behavior, partly because of our prior expectation about what "that kind of person" will say. We think that we already know what they will say when they talk, so we don't bother to listen. We do the same thing for Russians, Chinese, Palestinians, and South Africans, and for feminists, conservatives, and punks. We hear what we expect to hear, interpreting the words into meanings that make sense to us.

Semantic Differences   Part of the reason it's easy to misunderstand people from a different culture is due to expectations, and part of the problem lies in semantic differences—differences in word meanings. Because people have different life experiences, their ideas differ. When people with different life experiences use the same words, then understanding becomes very difficult.

Take the example of the sociologist who went to China and taught a course on "the family." As you're probably aware, the idea of "family" in China differs greatly from that of Western Europeans and Americans. The Chinese, who have practiced ancestor worship for centuries and who respect old people highly, have one set of experiences, attitudes, and values attached to the idea of family, whereas Americans and Western Europeans, who live in nuclear families often many miles from their nearest relatives, have another set of experiences, attitudes, and values attached to the idea of family. If two people from such very different backgrounds could come to any understanding on the topic of family, it would be a wonder. So assuming that both Chinese and Americans mean the same thing by the word "family" would be a very grave error of semantics.

To a lesser extent, the same thing happens within cultures. People in different parts of the United States have differing experiences, attitudes, and values although they speak the same language. Differences in ethnic background lead to different meanings for the same words. To someone in Mississippi "snow" is a wonderful and unusual experience, something to let school out for and to enjoy and revel in. In Buffalo, which may get over five feet of snow before Christmas, "snow" is a less exciting concept. And someone in Colorado who depends on the skiing industry for a living will have an even different orientation toward the fluffy white stuff. If we aren't aware that the same words can mean different things to different people, we may make serious mistakes in interpreting what we hear.

In all these ways—social rules, expectations, and distractions—listening can be a difficult task. Becoming an effective listener will depend partly on how well you can analyze the social conditions that affect your listening behaviors and not be trapped into ineffective listening habits.

Interference Number Four
Individual Psychological Factors Inhibit Effective Listening.

In addition to physical distractions and social conditions that interfere with successful listening, there are also individual factors that may interfere. These individual factors include bad listening habits, bad attitudes toward listening, and inappropriate emotional responses in the listening situation. While it may be difficult or impossible to eliminate physical distractions or to change social expectations, *psychological factors* may be remediable, once you recognize them. Attitudes and habits can be changed, although it takes time, patience, and a lot of practice.

Listening Habits   As already established, listening is a conscious, purposive action; it's not something that we can naturally do well. Like any other activity we learn, our listening behavior is largely habitual. We seldom think about what we are doing; we just listen. And some of our listening habits can be counterproductive; we can learn to listen badly as easily as we can learn to listen well. The problem is that unless we fail spectacularly we tend not even to think about our habitual actions. A driver may make that left-hand turn without signaling for years until the one time when the person following wasn't watching and an accident occurred. So we probably go on day by day listening fairly well, but missing out on a lot because we don't know what we are missing.

To illustrate this idea, let's take the example of horseback riding. If your parents bought you a pony and let you teach yourself to ride on that pony, you might come to think you were a pretty good rider. Chances are, though, there would be a lot of things about horseback riding that you wouldn't know because you had never been taught. Until you attended a horse show and saw what professional riders could do, you might never even know you were missing anything. Once you saw what was possible, you might be interested in taking lessons and learning how to ride better. But you would probably have picked up some bad habits that you would have to work very hard to change. Listening is not unlike horseback riding or playing the piano. You can learn by yourself and do a pretty good job, but systematic training would make the learning easier and teach you effective habits. Anyone who has tried to stop biting his or her finger-nails or smoking will tell you how hard it is to break bad habits.

Failure to Set a Goal   One of the more common failings in listening is the failure to set a goal for listening. If you don't know where you're going, any road will get you there. But if you need to get to a certain place at a particular time, you can't take just any road. You have to take the best road. It's the same thing with listening. If you're not going to have to know or do anything, it doesn't matter how you listen. But if you're going to have to act on the basis of what you heard, you have to know what you're listening for. Often when students begin college and have to take notes from lectures they have a hard time. They try to write down everything the professor says, because they don't know what's important. It takes several weeks (months?) of practice to learn how to take notes effec-tively—to learn how to listen for the main points. Or when someone begins a new job, he or she trys to remember everything about the job. Again it takes some time to learn what's important and what can safely be left to do later. New students and new employees need to listen for main points to help them pick out the most important ideas.

There are other times when knowing what to listen for is important. If you're buying a new car, every salesperson will tell you their automobile is the best. You have to decide which one is right for you. In order to do that you have to listen to what evidence each salesperson uses to support his or her argument for the product. Otherwise you may end up buying the wrong car because you liked one salesperson better than another, or because one salesperson was more glib or enthusiastic. Listening for evidence is another listening skill that you have to learn. Listeners who know what they are listening for and how to listen for something in particular are much more successful than listeners who can't set themselves specific goals.

A second related problem with listening is setting inappropriate goals for listening. Going back to the example of the new college student, we find that many freshmen try to listen just for the facts and write them all down. Instead, they should begin by listening for the organizational pattern and the main ideas of the lecture. Once students understand the organizational pattern, the main ideas will be clear. And once the main ideas are clear, the facts will all fit into place like pieces of a puzzle. But without understanding the organizational pattern and the main points, students will not see the connections between the facts and will not be able to remember or understand them. It's like trying to memorize a string of nonsense syllables. It's very difficult unless you make up a story or rhyme to remember them by. The story is like the organizational pattern, and the main ideas are the events in the story. Once you know the story and the events, you can remember the details. To understand something, then, you have to learn to listen for the pattern and the main ideas.

Listening for Feelings   In business, people often make the mistake of listening for facts when they should be paying attention to feelings. The way someone says something can often be as important or more important than exactly what that person says. A salesperson has to know, for example, when to talk to customers and when to listen, when to push the product and when to back off and let customers make up their minds. You can probably remember when a pushy salesperson kept giving you the hard sell when you had no real intention of buying. Maybe you went away and never came back, even if you were thinking of buying, because you didn't like the salesperson's style. Emotion is a very important (maybe the most important) element of persuasion, and learning to listen for feelings is an important skill for anyone who has to work with the public. Listening for feelings is a very important part of a supervisor's repertoire of behaviors. Dissatisfied or disgruntled workers will not do as good a job as satisfied workers. Sometimes listening to employees and understanding their point of view, even if you don't have the power to change the situation, can lead to a better work atmosphere. Supervisors who can identify and respond appropriately to what employees are feeling will be more effective at their job than supervisors who can't or will not.

Listening for the Facts   On the other hand, it's also possible to pay attention to feelings when you should be paying attention to the facts. People often have to work when they aren't feeling well or when they are under some emotional stress. People often have to go to work even if the bank just bounced a check or the car broke down or someone in their family is ill. The most useful thing fellow workers can do is to ignore the feelings and get the work done. People under emotional stress may be sharp tempered or gloomy even if they don't mean to be. Reacting to the emotional content of what they say will only exacerbate the situation and cause more problems. People who have to deal with customer complaints have to learn to acknowledge customers' feelings but not to reciprocate. They try to get the facts so they can make a determination of the merits of the case. If they paid attention to the feelings, they would soon be upset themselves and no work would get done.

One listening goal that's almost never productive is listening to refute the other person's argument. We all know people who love to argue; they listen to your words in order to twist them around and then try to make you look foolish. Instead of listening to the sense of what's being said, they interpret everything they hear in terms of their own arguments. Debaters do this to make points, but in real life it's a very frustrating experience and seldom leads to any constructive outcome. It's a very bad listening habit.

Bad Listening Habits   Some other bad habits are pretending to listen, interrupting the speaker, finishing the other person's sentence, jumping to conclusions, and changing the subject. Pretending to listen may start out very innocently. You find yourself stuck with some bore at a party and you can't get away gracefully, so you pretend to listen. Or maybe one of your fellow workers complains endlessly about the same old thing, so you just quit listening. Family members often only pretend to listen to each other, assuming they already know what's going to be said. It's like having a switch in your head that you can turn off and on. The problem is that sometimes the person you're pretending to listen to may say something significant and you will have missed it. Maybe that bore at the party knows where to get tickets to the bowl game. Or, maybe one of the other people in the office has information about an important administrative change that will affect your job. If you have developed a habit of turning off when that person talks, you will miss important information that might have been very useful to you. Turning people off can sometimes save your sanity, but making a habit of it can sometimes cause you grief.

We have all had the experience of talking to someone who kept interrupting us in the middle of a sentence or a story. Although we are less likely to remember when we did it ourselves, we have probably all been guilty of this behavior sometimes, too. What's the effect when someone interrupts you in the middle of a thought? You become frustrated, then angry, and then you just quit trying to communicate. People who interrupt you sometimes finish the sentence for you; whether or not they guess correctly, it's no fun for you. Maybe they say something like, "Yeah, I know just what you mean. . . ." although they don't know what you meant to say. Whether the person who interrupted finished the sentence for you, or assumed he or she knew what you were going to say and responded incorrectly, the relationship was affected and communication ceased. Listeners who interrupt often misinterpret what was said (or what was meant) and they can seriously damage the relationship between the speaker and listener. This kind of interchange is often funny on television; it's the basis for most of the situation comedies. Gracie Allen was a master of the genre. But in real life it can cause serious misunderstandings between people.

Bad Attitudes in Listening   There are also some attitudes toward listening that can cause problems. Many people, for example, will decide beforehand whether the topic is going to be interesting or dull and then will act on their preconceptions. This is a hazard not only to college students, but also on the job and in personal relationships. Maybe you have a friend who has an interest you don't share—rugby or microcomputers or chess or cooking. When your friend starts to talk about that topic, you sigh or groan or just quit listening. Not only do you lose an opportunity to learn something new, but you may seriously affect the relationship as well. Deciding that chemistry or English or anthropology will be a boring class will make it much more difficult for you to learn the material and get a good grade in the course. If you decide a topic will not be interesting, you will automatically pay less attention and your listening will be less effective.

A related attitude is deciding that a topic will be too difficult. This is a perfect example of self-defeating behavior. If you think mathematics or statistics or music or art is going to be too difficult, you will probably find that it is. You will not listen as carefully or effectively, and you will find indeed that the subject is beyond you. Maybe you have decided that learning to use the office computer or word processor is too complex; you will never be able to do it. The problem usually is that someone else will not feel the topic is too difficult and that person will achieve what you failed to achieve. So they succeed where you failed, and you didn't even really try. That's not to say that no subjects are difficult or that you will not find yourself having difficulties learning new things sometimes. It just seems foolish to start out with the attitude that something will be too difficult and handicap yourself before you begin.

One final attitude that can interfere with successful listening is listening for what you expect to hear. A good example of this is when you were in high school and the counselor (or even worse, the principal) called you into the office. You probably went through a whole laundry list of all the things you had done that could have gotten you in trouble. And then the counselor (or principal) informed you that you were eligible for the scholarship, or had been chosen to go on a trip, or something else that was wonderful and unexpected. It probably took you a while to respond, since you had expected to hear something quite different.

Listening for what you expect to hear can also be a problem in personal relationships. We all play out scenes in our heads between ourselves and the people important to us, imagining what would happen if we said or did a certain thing. But if we act on the basis of the imaginary scenario we can get in real trouble. Let's take a simple story to illustrate what could happen if someone listens for what he or she expects to hear instead of keeping an open mind. George and Martha have been planning a vacation to Bermuda for the last three years. They have set the date, made the reservations, and arranged for someone to watch the house and take care of the dog. Then three days before they are scheduled to leave, one of the other lawyers in the office has an emergency appendectomy and Martha has to stay to take over that colleague's court cases. All the way home from work she imagines what George will say when she tells him. "He will be furious. . . . He will say that the damn job is more important to me than he is. . . . He will say he's going without me. . . . He will say this is the last time. . . ." By the time she gets home Martha is convinced that talking to George will be a waste of time and she's already mad at him for not understanding her dilemma. Martha may not even give George a chance, if she only listens for what she expects to hear. "I know what you're going to say," she may start out, "but it's not my fault." Now poor George is on the defensive, accused of something he didn't even do. By assuming that he will react in a certain way, she forces him into the position of reacting that way; all as a result of failing to listen with an open mind.

Emotional Responses to Listening   The story of Martha and George leads naturally into the last category of problems that interfere with listening effectiveness: Emotional responses can interfere with listening. Although all emotional responses affect listening to some degree, there are four particular problem areas. The first area has already been discussed in this chapter—the difficulty in listening attentively to someone of a lower social status. We just don't take them seriously. You can remember from your childhood that you seldom listened seriously to your younger sisters and brothers. They were just kids. Executives may not listen seriously to employees; they have a different sets of priorities. "I just don't want to hear it" is the typical response to communication from a social inferior, especially when that communication involves a problem of some kind. If someone says that to you consistently, you will just stop trying. The nonlistener loses an important source of information by allowing an emotional response to color his or her behavior.

Another emotional response that's really hard to overcome is not listening to someone you don't like. You will probably try to avoid meeting someone you don't like, but sometimes it just isn't possible. You may not like your supervisor or manager, but you need the job. You may not like your colleagues, but you have to work with them on committees or projects. You may not like someone on the bowling team or someone in the computer users' group, but the benefits of belonging to the group outweigh the aggravation you have to put up with. Your defense will be to ignore the person you don't like. You will not listen to him. If it's your supervisor you can't stand, you may begin to pretend you're listening, while in your head you're running a Walter Mitty routine of what you would like to be doing to him. If it's a colleague on a committee, you may begin daydreaming or you may decide to confront her and start a fight instead of listening. Whatever the response, it probably will not be productive listening.

Losing your temper is another emotional response that effectively shuts off listening. When you lose your temper, listening flies out the window. There may be times when it's strategic to lose your temper, but not when it's important that you pay attention to someone else. You can surely remember a time when you were trying to explain something to someone who was angry. You just had to go away and wait until that person cooled down enough to listen.

Finally, some people are put off by speech defects or accents that are different from their own. If you respond emotionally to the style of a person's speech, it's hard to pay attention to the words that person is saying. Maybe the person you're listening to stutters or has a lisp. You may become so embarrassed for him or her that you don't listen carefully. Some people react violently to southern accents, and some don't like accents of people from Brooklyn or the Bronx. Foreign accents are largely a matter of personal taste. Sometimes it's "in" to sound British, or "romantic" to sound French. Whatever the emotional response, it tends to detract from the sense of what the speaker is saying and listening is that much less effective.

Bad listening habits, bad attitudes toward listening, and emotional responses to the speaker are some psychological barriers to successful listening. By understanding yourself and your habits and attitudes, you can decide to become a more effective listener, to set appropriate goals, and to practice new skills and attitudes.

SUMMARY

In this chapter we defined and described the physical and psychological processes that make up listening. We explained how a particular range of vibrations in the air is received by the ear and processed into information in the brain. We distinguished between the physical process of hearing, which isn't under our conscious control and goes on continuously, and the psychological process of listening, which is partly under our conscious control and therefore is a selective and purposive process. We also listed and explained several kinds of factors that can interfere with successful listening. We identified physical, social, and psychological factors. Physical factors included distractions and physiological discomfort. Social factors included distractions from the presence of other people, social norms, social status, stereotyping, and semantic differences. Psychological factors included bad habits, bad attitudes, and emotional responses to the speaker. To the extent that you can identify when any of these factors is operating to constrain your listening effectiveness, you can take steps to eliminate or alleviate the effect and become a better listener. The rest of the book will be concerned with specific ways to improve listening behaviors.

SUGGESTED ACTIVITIES

1. Find a quiet place and sit down to listen for ten minutes. List all the sounds you can identify. Are there sounds you can't identify? Do the same exercise in a noisy place. Are there sounds you can't identify? Notice that when you concentrate on a specific sound, you stop hearing other sounds.

2. Sit for ten minutes in your room. Listen to identify all the different sounds you can hear in that ten minutes. How many of those sounds are you usually aware of and how many do you usually not hear?

3. Get a tape or a record in a language you don't speak, or listen to a foreign language radio program. What can you understand of what you hear? Can you identify the sex and/or age of the speakers? Can you identify the emotions portrayed by the speaker? Can you catch any of the meaning of the words? This exercise will help you understand the necessity of a shared code to convey meaning.

4. Keep a listening log of your listening behavior for three days. Get a small notebook and write down a summary of what you're doing every half hour. At the end of that three days, look over your log and see if you can find patterns of listening behavior. Are there particular people you have trouble listening to? Are there particular situations in which your listening is less effective? What factors do you think are affecting your listening?

REFERENCES AND RECOMMENDED READING

Bradley, Bert E. "Responsibilities of Receivers: Effective Listening." In *Speech Communication: The Credibility of Ideas* (4th Edition). Dubuque, IA: William C. Brown, 1984, pp. 32–42.

Denes, Peter B., and Elliot N. Pinson. *The Speech Chain: The Physics and Biology of Spoken Language.* Garden City, NY: Anchor Books/Doubleday, 1973.

Fry, Dennis. *Homo Loquens: Man as a Talking Animal.* Cambridge, MA: Cambridge University Press, 1977.

Gavin, Kathleen. *Listening by Doing.* Lincolnwood, IL: National Textbook, 1985.

Nichols, Ralph G. "Do We Know How to Listen? Practical Helps in a Modern Age." *The Speech Teacher* 18 (1961): 120.

Taylor, Anita, Teresa Rosegrant, Arthur Meyer, and B. Thomas Samples. "Listening." In *Communicating.* Englewood Cliffs, NJ: Prentice-Hall, 1986, pp. 133–163.

Watzlawick, Paul, J. H. Beavin, and D. D. Jackson. *Pragmatics of Human Behavior.* New York: W. W. Norton, 1969.

Young, J. Z. *Programs of the Brain.* New York: Oxford University Press, 1978.

Zolten, Joseph Jerome. *The Use of Premeditated Humor in Interpersonal Relationships.* Dissertation, The Pennsylvania State University, 1982.

chapter 3

Setting Goals for Listening

When you finish this chapter you should be able to:

1. Identify four main goals for listening.
2. Identify appropriate listening goals for specific situations.
3. Describe the criteria for a good goal statement.
4. Develop good listening goals.
5. Distinguish between primary and secondary listening goals.

When you have finished this chapter, you should be able to define these concepts:

1. goal setting
2. appropriate listening goals
3. good goal statement
4. primary listening goals

In the last chapter we considered some factors that interfere with listening. One of the most important barriers to listening is the lack of a specific goal. People who don't know what they are listening for will not do a very good job. There is an old story about a man who was looking around one dark night under the streetlight. A passerby asked if he had lost something.

"Yes, I lost my wallet," the man replied.
"Where did you lose it?" the passerby asked.

"In the alley over there," the man replied.

"But if you lost the wallet in the alley over there, why in heaven's name are you looking for it here?" asked the astounded passerby.

"Because there's no light there to look by," was the reply.

The same thing can happen with listening; if we don't specify what it is we need to find out and how to go about finding out we may waste our time listening in the wrong way.

In this chapter we identify four general goals for listening: (1) listening to understand, (2) listening to maintain relationships, (3) listening to make a decision, and (4) listening to enjoy. By choosing one of these main goals, we can learn to focus our listening on a specific purpose and achieve that purpose.

LISTENING GOALS

To illustrate the differences among these four different kinds of listening, we can take the example of a concert. You might think that there would be only one kind of listening going on at a concert—listening to enjoy—but in fact all four kinds of listening occur there. Usually each person at the concert has only one primary listening goal, but different people at the concert have different goals.

Listening to Enjoy and Understand

Most of the people who attend the concert probably have the goal of enjoyment in mind. They bought tickets to hear this particular group or this particular kind of music. But there are other people present at any concert who have other goals in mind. At any particular concert, there is probably a small percentage of people who have never heard this group or this kind of music before. They are people who came because they wanted a new experience. "We've never listened to bluegrass music before; let's go and check it out." These people may be hoping to enjoy the music, but they are more likely just trying to understand it. Japanese music, Jamaican steel bands, opera, ragtime piano, music by a new composer, or a new rock group are all kinds of music that people might want to go and listen to in order to discover if they liked it. So at any concert, there will probably be many people who are listening to enjoy and some people who are listening to understand.

You know, I was at the Arts Festival last year and I happened to go by the fiddling contest they have on Saturdays. I don't like country music much, but that fiddling was real interesting. I didn't know there were so many different ways to play the fiddle. If they have it next year, I think I'll go back again.

Listening to Decide

There will also be people at a concert who are listening to decide about the quality of the music. The music critics and reviewers will be listening to critique the performance for the newspapers and magazines covering that kind of music. If the performance is being broadcast or recorded, there will also be technicians who listen to decide how they can best represent the music on the air or on tape. This is a completely different kind of listening from either of the other two. People who listen to decide must take action based on their listening: write a review or make a recording. These people pay careful attention to preselected aspects of the music, whether or not they enjoy the music.

Listening to Maintain Relationships

Finally there will be people at the concert listening to maintain relationships: The people in the musical group have to listen carefully to one another to be sure they are playing what they should be playing at the right time, in the right tempo, at the right pitch, and so on. If you have ever played in a musical group you know how important it is to coordinate what you're doing with what everyone else is doing. If there is a director, that person listens to maintain the balance of relationships among all the performers. Just for fun sometime, stop listening for a while and watch the nonverbal behavior of the members of the group. A trio or quartet is best for this exercise. You will notice that the individual performers execute a kind of dance movement while they are playing, keeping in time and watching each other for cues as to what's coming next. By listening carefully to one another, they maintain their relationships with one another and create music together.

> In our barbershop quartet, every person has to know all the words and all the notes exactly right. If one of us makes a mistake the director is all over us. We have to have the songs perfect for any performance, but we can only do that by being together with everyone else. Someone who makes a mistake isn't chosen for the next performance; if they keep making mistakes they are asked to leave the group. You have to have a good ear to be in a barbershop quartet.

You probably will have noticed that none of these listening goals exists alone. In order to enjoy something, you have to understand it first. If you have friends who listen to different kinds of music from what you listen to, you may wonder, "How can they listen to that noise? It makes my head ache!" Someone else has probably made the same remark about the kind of music you listen to. And your reply was, "But you don't understand it. Just listen to how the. . . ." The more you learn about music, the more you can appreciate it. That's what music appreciation classes are about; you learn to understand many different kinds of music in order to learn to enjoy them.

And in order to make a judgment about something—is it a good one or a bad one—you will have to understand it first. Music critics don't have to be great musicians, but they do have to understand how music is made and what the standards for good music are. We don't ask taxi drivers to evaluate musical performance, and we don't ask music critics about the traffic patterns in a city. Knowledge is the basis of judgment in any field. By the same token, it's unlikely that people would become expert enough to become critics unless they really enjoyed what they were listening to. Enjoyment is an important part of the critical process, too.

Listening to maintain relationships is also related to understanding and enjoyment. In order to maintain any kind of relationship, you have to know what that relationship should be. In order to play loud enough, for example, you have to know how loud is enough. Or to play in the right key, you have to know something about pitch. In order to remain friendly with other people, you have to know what kinds of behaviors they look on as being friendly. If you're accustomed to teasing your friends and you meet someone who looks on teasing as hostile behavior, you will not remain on good terms very long. And relationships are usually based on mutual enjoyment of each other's company and of mutual interests.

Each of these general goals for listening—understanding, making decisions, enjoying, maintaining relationships—is related to the other goals. But in any particular situation it's important to be able to determine which goal is most appropriate. Most people usually can only do one thing at a time, so you have to decide whether you should be listening to understand, to make a decision, to maintain a relationship, or to enjoy. If you don't know what you should be doing, you're like a ship without a rudder; you will not have any control over what happens and you're likely to run aground or be overwhelmed by the waves. In this chapter we consider what's involved with each of these listening goals and how to decide on an appropriate goal.

GOAL-SETTING

In this section on goal-setting we define what a goal is, teach you to distinguish a good goal from a poor one, and demonstrate how to define listening goals for yourself.

What Is a Goal?

Goals are statements that specify what you want to accomplish. They are statements that describe the world as you would like it to be. We set goals because we aren't satisfied with things as they are and we want to make changes. If you have enrolled in a communication class, you probably have set yourself a goal to improve your understanding of the communication process and improve your own communication performance. If you're reading this book, you probably have set yourself a goal to understand the listening process better and become a better listener.

But there is a difference between saying how you want things to be and setting goals. The difference lies in how specific you get about what it is you want to happen. For example, you might say, "I want to become a better communicator." The statement sounds rather like a goal, but in fact it's probably more like wishful thinking. From the statement itself there is no way to determine what would be different if you became a "better communicator," or how you might go about becoming one. Often students in public speaking classes report they want to become "less nervous" or "more confident." But without statements about what more confident might look like or what steps to take to become more confident, the statement remains worthless as a goal. A goal statement must fulfill these requirements:

1. A goal statement specifies the end result.
2. A goal statement specifies conditions.
3. A goal statement allows measurement.

How Do I Recognize a Good Goal?

So what would a goal statement about communication look like? To illustrate, we build a goal statement from the initial formless wish: "I want to become a better communicator." To specify the end result, we change the statement to say:

I want to learn how to deliver a public speech.

That makes the statement more concrete, because now we have specified a behavior instead of the amorphous *better communicator.* You will notice, of course, that there are many possible interpretations of what better communicator might mean. Instead of public speaking, we might set goals like these:

I want to learn how to initiate, maintain, and terminate a conversation.

I want to learn how to give clear instructions.

In fact, to describe what you mean by better communicator you may have to set yourself several more specific goals. By deciding what behaviors make up a better communicator you will have made it easier actually to achieve what you wanted.

We have also said that a *good goal statement* specifies conditions. The statement "I want to learn how to deliver a public speech" might mean anything from giving a sales pitch for Girl Scout cookies to delivering the State of the Union message. It's unlikely that you had either of these two contingencies in mind, so we will have to be more specific:

I want to learn how to make a report to the student government on changing the grading system.

That statement specifies under what conditions the speech will take place, which also makes it more likely that you will be able to decide if you were successful. The statement satisfies all the preceding criteria. You will notice again that the phrase "give a public speech" could also have been interpreted differently. You might have meant "give the treasurer's report at the school board meeting," "deliver a sermon at church," "deliver a campaign speech," or a number of other possibilities. If you have a broader understanding of public speech you may have to specify more than one goal statement. But it's better to be more specific than too general, because if you're too general you will not be able to tell whether or not you were successful (Criterion 3).

Let's look at some other examples of good and bad goals. Since this is a book about listening, let's look at some listening goals.

POOR: I want to learn to appreciate music.
GOOD: I want to learn to recognize the individual instruments in an orchestra when I hear them in a concert.

POOR: I want to learn to understand people.
GOOD: I want to learn to recognize voice cues that indicate emotions when people are speaking to me.

You should think of other possible listening goals and see whether they meet the criteria for specifying the end result, allowing for measurement, and specifying conditions. Try making these poor goal statements into more specific goal statements:

POOR: I want to learn to be more sensitive to other people's feelings.
GOOD: _____
       _____

POOR: I want to know how to pick the best candidate.
GOOD: _____
       _____

How Do I Learn to Set Goals for Myself?

Knowing what a good goal looks like will help you specify good listening goals, but it will not necessarily lead you to set the most appropriate listening goals in a particular situation. First you need to know that setting yourself goals for listening isn't really your first priority in any situation. Your first priority is to decide why you're listening. Listening goals are really subsidiary or secondary goals in the service of a larger or primary goal. You listen to accomplish another purpose; you don't listen just to listen.

Your first task, then, is to identify what your primary goals are and only then to decide what listening goals you want to set for yourself. To illustrate this concept, let's take some examples.

For the first example, let's assume you're a student in a public speaking course. You may set yourself the goal of making a good grade, probably an A or a B. Your main goal, then, would be as follows:

I want to achieve a good mark (A or B) in the class.

But in order to achieve that goal, you will have to specify what it will take to get a good mark. You have to discover what work you will have to do at what level of competence to earn an A or a B. You can discover this information by reading the syllabus and listening to the instructor's description of the course or by asking the instructor what the requirements are. As a subgoal of your first goal, you may then decide to do the following:

> I will determine what level of competence in what activities will enable me to earn a grade of A or B in this class.

To achieve this subgoal, clearly you will have to listen to understand the requirements for the course. You might then set yourself a listening goal like the following:

> I will listen to identify the requirements for a grade of A or B in this class.

You will see that the particular listening goal is designed to help you achieve your main goal. In order to discover the requirements for the course, you have to listen to understand. Since this is a public speaking course, let's assume that to earn a good grade you have to give three speeches at the level of A or B work. Now you will have to set yourself another goal:

> I will determine what the criteria for an A or a B speech are.

And to achieve this subgoal, you will have to set yourself another listening goal:

> I will listen to identify the criteria for an A or a B speech.

There are several ways to identify what the criteria are for an A or a B speech. The instructor should be able to list the criteria, but it's often hard to understand what those criteria mean in actual practice. You need to see and hear several speeches in order to be able to judge what work is considered A or B work. So you may decide that you can learn by listening to other students' speeches. You set yourself this goal:

> I will evaluate my fellow students' speeches to discover what the instructor considers A or B work.

In order to achieve that goal, you must listen to the speeches as though you were the instructor assigning a grade to the speech. The following listening goal will help you achieve that goal:

> I will listen to my fellow students' speeches to decide what grade the teacher would assign.

Now you have set yourself a different listening goal. When you are applying the teacher's criteria to a particular speech, you're listening to decide whether that performance met those criteria. Listening to decide is different from listening to understand. When you were listening to understand, you listened for specific ideas and facts to remember them. When you listen to decide on a grade for the speeches, you're comparing what you heard with what you know about the standards for a good speech. When you listen to decide, you listen to evaluate and judge. You will also judge your own success based on the goal you set for yourself.

To illustrate this point, we invent three hypothetical students: Oliver, Louise, and Addie. Each student listens to the speeches in class with a different goal. Oliver is listening to the speeches to enjoy them; he's less than entirely serious about this class. Louise is listening to the speeches to learn something about the topics the students are speaking on. She's interested in learning about all kinds of new and different things. And Addie is listening to decide whether the speeches are good or bad. Addie wants to get an A in the class, and she's figuring out what kind of speech will earn her that grade.

You notice that each person's primary goal is different in the class: Oliver intends to enjoy the class, Louise wants to learn something new, and Addie wants to get an A. Although none of these goals really excludes the others, most people choose to emphasize one or the other. What we want to point out is that the outcome of choosing any one of these strategies will affect (1) what you will end up with and (2) how you will measure your own success.

Oliver is set on enjoying the class and enjoying the speeches. When a round of speeches is over, Oliver will be able to tell you which ones he liked and which ones he didn't like. He probably will not be able to tell you what the speeches were about or anything else about the speeches. Louise will be able to tell you what the speeches were about, and she will probably have specific information about some of the topics that interested her. If Louise liked some speeches more than others, it will probably be because she understood them better or because the topic appealed to her. Addie, on the other hand, will be able to tell you what makes a good speech and a poor speech and which speeches met the criteria for good speeches in this class. She may like the good speeches better, or she may not even be able to say which ones she liked. She may not remember what they were about either.

How Do I Judge Whether I Was Successful?

In all three of the preceding cases the students focused on different aspects of the speeches while they were listening. Oliver, interested in enjoying, probably noticed aspects of the delivery. He probably liked the speeches where the speaker was lively and fluent, having a good time speaking. Louise probably paid most attention to the information given in the speeches, disregarding the delivery and the technical structure of the speech. Addie probably concentrated on specific technical aspects of speechmaking, including delivery. You might even say that these three different people with their different goals heard three different rounds of speeches. Knowing how listening goals affect what we pay attention to helps explain how different people can have such different opinions of the same performance.

One important aspect of setting goals is determining to what extent you were successful in achieving your goals. This determination is closely tied to the goal you specified for yourself. Addie wouldn't, for example, decide she was a successful listener by whether or not she enjoyed the class. It wasn't her purpose to enjoy the class. She would decide if she were successful by whether she got an A in the course. Oliver, however, set himself the goal of enjoying the class, so it's not appropriate for him to determine his success by his grade. It shouldn't matter to him whether he got an A or a C; his only concern should be his enjoyment of the class. And Louise can't really use her grade as a way of judging her success either, because getting a particular grade wasn't her goal. She was in the class to learn new and interesting things—to understand. She will measure her achievement by the amount of information she gained from the class.

We could avoid frustration if we were more specific about our goals in particular situations. How many of your friends set out to enjoy classes or to get through them with as little work as possible and then are dissatisfied because their grades reflect these goals? Or, maybe you know people who set out to get a perfect 4.0 grade point average, and then complain because they don't enjoy school? Both kinds of people are choosing to measure their success by inappropriate standards. The standards we choose to measure success have to be directly related to the goals we chose. And it's important to be clear on what our goals are, so we can measure our own success.

If you're unsure about what your listening goals should be in a particular situation, you might ask yourself the question, "What will I be expected to do when I have finished listening?" The answer to that question should lead you to an appropriate goal. You should choose a goal by specifying what you want the outcome to be and the conditions under which you will act. It's not always a good idea to set yourself the goal of getting an A in a class, because you don't give yourself grades. In any class, it's the teacher who makes the decisions on grading; so the grade you get is really out of your own control.

It's better to set a goal that you have some control over. It might even be a better idea to try for the highest grade you *can* get instead of trying to get an A. You will still listen to discover what the standards are and what a good performance looks like, and you will be able to judge to what extent you met those standards and achieved that performance given your own limitations. Not all of us can be football stars, math whizes, or great singers. But that doesn't mean we can't try our best and perform well. Good goal-setting can help you perform better and be more realistic in your appraisal of your own performance. You have a better chance of getting what you want when you know what that is, can figure out how to get it, and recognize when you have it.

SUMMARY

In this chapter we illustrated how choosing a listening goal can help you become a more successful listener. We defined four general listening goals: (1) listening to understand, (2) listening to make a decision, (3) listening to maintain relationships, and (4) listening for enjoyment. We described how to decide on appropriate listening goals and how to distinguish good goals from poor goals. We illustrated how the choice of a specific goal will lead you to appropriate behavior to achieve that goal. And we explained how to measure your success by referring back to your specific goal. Now we are ready to address more comprehensively each of the four main listening goals we have identified.

SUGGESTED ACTIVITIES

1. Identify situations in which your primary goals might be (1) to listen to understand, (2) to listen to maintain a relationship, (3) to listen to decide, and (4) to listen for enjoyment.

2. Pick one of your other classes or a work situation. Identify what your overall goal in that class or work situation is. Then identify specific listening goals that will help you achieve your overall goal.

3. What do you want to be doing in five years? What main goal will you have to achieve to be doing that? What subgoals will you have to set in order to achieve your main goal? What listening skills will be most useful in achieving your goals?

REFERENCES AND RECOMMENDED READING

Donaghy, William C. "Listening." In *The Interview: Skills and Applications.* Dallas, TX: Scott, Foresman, 1984, pp. 151–171.

Goodall, H. Lloyd. *Creating Reality.* Dubuque, IA: William C. Brown, 1983.

Lucas, Stephen E. *The Art of Public Speaking.* New York: Random House, 1983.

Mager, Robert F. *Goal Analysis.* Belmont, CA: Pitman Management and Training, 1972.

Sigband, Norman B. *Communication for Management and Business* (3rd Edition). Dallas, TX: Scott, Foresman, 1982.

Verderber, Rudolph F., and Kathleen S. Verderber. *Interact* (3rd Edition). Belmont, CA: Wadsworth, 1984.

Wood, Julia T. *Human Communication.* New York: Holt, Rinehart and Winston, 1982.

chapter *4*

Listening for Understanding

When you have finished reading this chapter you should be able to:

1. Explain the importance of listening to understand in personal as well as in public situations: in families, in communities, and at work.
2. List and describe four important components of listening to understand.
3. Define and describe how those four important components affect our understanding of what we hear.
4. Explain how to consider each of those four components when we listen to understand.
5. Name and explain seven common organizational patterns.

When you have finished reading this chapter you should be able to describe these important concepts:

1. context
2. paralanguage
3. organizational patterns
4. abstraction
5. onstage and backstage behaviors
6. nonverbal communication

Since listening to understand seems to be at least partially the basis for the other listening goals, we begin with the topic of listening to understand. Listening is indeed the basic way to learn. Although some of our learning is achieved by trial and error, learning by trial and error is inefficient and often dangerous. "Once burned, twice shy" is the old saying, and children who have been burned quickly learn to heed the warning "Hot!" After the first time they are more likely to listen to warnings before they get hurt.

Once children have learned language, they seem to have an insatiable appetite for new words and ideas. They work their way from what things are called to how things work to why things happen. While we sometimes think they never stop talking, in fact, children spend a great deal of time listening. "Little pitchers have big ears," is a warning that children are always listening to what's going on around them, even when we would rather they weren't. Parents are often astounded at the bits of knowledge their children pick up (and are likely to repeat in inappropriate contexts). Art Linkletter made quite a good business of this propensity of children to listen and repeat what they have heard with his television show and book *Kids Say the Darndest Things.*

LISTENING TO LEARN

The most obvious examples of listening to understand occur in school or on the job where we are learning new information formally. Much of school time is taken up with listening to lectures or discussing school subjects. The time in between formal classes is spent listening to keep up with the current music, styles, and social activities. On the job, we have to listen to find out what we need to know to get the work done. Listening at work is more or less formal: telephone calls, briefings, reports, interviews, conversations. In all these situations, we are listening for information in order to understand what has happened in the past, what's happening now, and what will happen in the future so we can respond appropriately.

We also spend time listening to understand in situations that are not specifically defined as learning situations. Since the environment we live in is always changing, we have to spend a great deal of our lives listening to find out what we need to know just to get along. We are constantly meeting new people, finding ourselves in new situations, having to learn new ways of doing things. This is true not only for children who are constantly outgrowing their clothes and changing their hairstyles and attitudes, but also for adults who grow older, change jobs, get married, have children, get divorced, or move to new communities. Even if they keep the same job in the same community, chances are the community will change and the people they work with and socialize with will change with the community. Businesses close and new establishments take their place; employment patterns change; schools expand or consolidate.

> What happened to the shoe repair place? I went by the other day and the whole complex had been torn down. I asked somebody and he said he thought the land had been bought by a big department store. If they put in a new store, the traffic will be impossible. This area has changed so much in the last ten years, you wouldn't recognize it.

We also spend a lot of time keeping up with our friends' and families' lives, learning about what they are doing. This kind of listening to understand includes more than just keeping up with the facts; it includes listening to understand feelings. It's not enough to learn that your sister has a new job; you want to know how she likes it. Is it going to be a good move, or will she run into problems? Does she like the work, the people, the location? Often this kind of listening involves more than listening to the words. It involves listening to the tone of voice, noticing an expression or posture, or listening for what the other person *isn't* saying. Often when someone stops talking about something she used to talk about, it means there is some kind of trouble.

Listening to understand feelings is a complex and difficult task, and it isn't something that's easy to learn. To understand other people's feelings, you have to know how they think, what they value, and how they react to other people and to the world. Often what people don't say is an important clue to their real feelings.

> I always know when Kevin's team is losing. When he comes home from a game, he doesn't say anything. He just goes into his room and shuts the door. It's no use to try talking to him about it. I just wait until he gets over it.

Unfortunately, most people overestimate their own listening abilities. At listening workshops when people are asked to estimate how efficient they are at listening, they usually estimate that they will remember 75 or 80 percent of what they hear. In fact, they can usually remember less than 25 percent of what they hear. This chapter describes the process of listening to understand in more detail and provide some guidelines to improve your abilities to listen for understanding. When you have finished this chapter you should be better able to avoid misunderstanding what you hear and to remember what you listen to.

FOUR COMPONENTS OF LISTENING TO UNDERSTAND

The four most important things to remember when you listen to understand are that (1) you must pay attention to the context of what is being said, (2) you must listen to identify the feelings of the speaker, (3) you must understand the organizational pattern and the ideas that are being presented, and (4) you must be careful in your interpretation of silence. In all these areas an understanding of the nature of language and of human behavior will help you to listen more effectively.

Importance of Context

Maybe we should start by illustrating some of the things that can go wrong and lead to misunderstandings. You have probably had the experience of having something you said taken out of context and misunderstood. This often happens in families when two members of the family discuss a third member who's not present and the conversation gets reported to everyone else. Or it can happen at work when someone overhears part of a conversation and reports that part as the whole story. "The management is planning to shut down the whole plant in Springfield! I heard them talking about it at the luncheon meeting!" When in fact the discussion was about moving to larger quarters and vacating the old building in Springfield. This is, of course, one of the classic ways rumors get started, and it's a perennial problem for all of us. Politicians are particularly susceptible to this kind of distortion, and they very soon learn how to speak without saying anything they could be held accountable for. Public figures hate to be quoted out of context, so they often stick to generalizations that mean nothing at all.

Importance of Feelings

You're also aware that the tone of voice is an important clue to the meaning of what's being said. "Harry is a character," may be a statement of admiration, disgust, or wonder, or it may mean that Harry is acting in the school play. It all depends on how it's said. Sometimes people say things in jest that are taken seriously, and sometimes people say things in all seriousness when listeners believe they are jesting. Facial expressions, body gestures, and timing are all elements that can modify the meaning of the words that are spoken. These elements of communication are called paralanguage by people who study them. Irony and sarcasm rely on paralanguage for their effect. Identifying what people feel is an important part of listening for understanding.

And then there is language itself, which is complex enough without the added problems of context and paralanguage. Most words have more than one meaning, so it's possible to misunderstand someone because you have chosen a meaning that was different from what that person intended. Or it may be that someone has used words with which you aren't familiar. Even familiar words have both denotational meanings—the thing the word refers to—and connotational meanings—the feelings associated with that word. Although you can find the denotational meaning of a word in the dictionary, connotations are often personal and unpredictable. Using a word without understanding its connotational meaning can cause untold confusion. The confusion can be amusing, as when a foreign student reported he had spent the weekend "watching magazines." Or the consequences can be more serious, as President Carter found out on his trip to Poland. His translator made an unfortunate choice of words and translated the sentence, "I have just left the United States" into Polish as "I have just emigrated from the United States." The Polish audience was understandably astounded and troubled. The symbolic nature of language provides ample opportunity for misunderstanding.

> Last semester Mary and I signed up for a course in basic computer programming. We thought it was a course for beginners. You know, turn on the computer, put in the disk, take the disk out, and so on. It turned out that BASIC is a computer language, and the course was about actually writing computer programs. We felt obsolete!

What's more dangerous because it's more subtle is the way words that refer only to conceptions or ideas are indistinguishable from words that refer to concrete objects. "Intelligence quotient" is only an abstraction that refers to a score on a particular pencil-and-paper test, but people often treat IQ as though it were a physical quality of the person who owns it, like blue eyes or brown hair. Personality, attitude, and character are other such *abstractions* as are government, corporation, and school. Do the buildings in Washington, DC, make up the federal government? Is it the people who hold office? Or, is it the rules by which we are obliged to live our lives and conduct our business? None of these things, of course, constitutes the federal government, but we sometimes behave as though they did.

> I was trying to study the other night and my little brother kept bugging me. "Who's the Pentagon?" he wanted to know. "It's not a person," I replied, "it's a building." "But the TV man said the Pentagon said the Russians were more prepared," he replied. "That's dumb. How can a building talk?"

Importance of Word Order

Another problem in understanding may occur when the person you are listening to gets things out of order, so you can't understand what he or she is talking about. Remember the last time a 10-year-old tried to tell you what happened in a movie? Or when someone who really understood computers tried to explain a simple computer task; he knew so much about it he couldn't remember to translate back to your level. Understanding the organizational pattern of a message will help you avoid misunderstanding as will understanding the complex levels on which language works.

Importance of Silence

Finally there is the problem of what wasn't said. We tend to think of silence as the absence of speech, but silence serves a number of important functions in communication. There are social rules for who can talk and who can't. "Children should be seen and not heard." Silence can signal agreement or disagreement. Silence between two people who hate each other can be deafening. And often it may be the things that aren't said that are most meaningful. This occurs in personal life; it's very difficult sometimes to tell someone else your deepest feelings. And it can happen at work. "Knowledge is power," and when information isn't shared it can have important consequences. Hoarding information is a kind of power play that some people use to control other people. Figuring out what wasn't said and interpreting the meaning of the silence is also an important listening skill.

In all four of these areas there are ways to improve your listening skills. In this chapter we explore each of these areas and provide guidelines for improvement.

LISTENING IN CONTEXT

You are probably already aware that what people will say to their friends in the local pub and what they will swear to in court aren't necessarily the same. This example illustrates the importance of context in interpreting what we hear.

The context in which communication takes place can significantly affect what information is available to a listener and how that information should be interpreted. *Context* includes both the physical surroundings and the social occasion. The social occasion can be defined as the people who are present and the purpose for those people to be together at that time and place. The physical surroundings may contain distractions that affect what it's possible to hear, or the ambience or atmosphere of the place may encourage a particular kind of talk and discourage other kinds of talk. In order to understand what's being said and what's not being said, we need to understand the context in the particular communication situation.

Erving Goffman (1959) explored the concept of context through the metaphor of theater. He noted that people's behavior differs when they are in public situations *(onstage behavior)* and when they are in private situations *(backstage behavior)*. At work, employees have one way of behaving when the boss is around and another way of behaving when the boss is elsewhere. Their behavior includes what they will say, so employees have one way of speaking to authorities and another way of speaking among themselves. It's the same at home; when it's "just the family" family members behave differently from the way they behave when visitors are present. Families who may disagree enthusiastically among themselves often present a united front to the world. Understanding what someone is saying, then, may depend on the context—onstage or backstage—of the conversation.

> I teach a course in the evening session this semester, and I got to class early one day. There were about five or six students already there, and I sat at a table in the back of the room. Chris came breezing in and sat at the other end of the table. He leaned over to his friend Brad and whispered very loudly, "Remember the accident was Sunday night, not Saturday. This paper was due Monday and it's late." There was silence in the room. Chris looked around and saw me watching him. "Oh, God," he said, "I guess I blew it." "I guess you did," I replied.

You may be able to understand the importance of context better by imagining that you have won one of those once-in-a-lifetime all-expense-paid trips to the resort of your dreams, say, Paris. You flew to Paris and spent seven exciting days and nights exploring the Left Bank and the Champs Elysées, shopping and visiting museums, and tasting the famous nightlife of this magnificent city. When you arrived exhausted and broke back home, you had to tell all your friends and family and colleagues about your trip.

But you didn't find yourself telling everyone the same story. The stories you told your parents about the museums and cafés weren't the same as those you told your buddies about the nightlife of Paris. Some of your friends were interested in the shops and fashions; those stories would have bored some of your other friends to death. In fact, you found yourself tailoring the account of your trip to the interests and expectations of the people who were listening to you. A stranger who collected all the different stories you told might even believe that several different people had taken several different trips to Paris. But in all likelihood none of the people you talked with was aware that you had edited your account for them.

Effects of Context

While most people are aware of the effect of context on what they can say, very few of us seem to take into account that context also affects what other people tell us. We all seem to feel that whatever anyone tells us must be the truth or the whole story. We don't realize that other people may tailor what they say to accord with what they think we expect or wish to hear. As a student you quickly found out which excuses a teacher would accept as valid for not getting your work done on time. What you may not have known was that the teachers probably knew you were making up stories they would believe most of the time.

Researchers in human behavior have to be aware of the context in which they ask their questions, because that context will have important effects on the answers they receive. Researchers interested in finding out about work conditions in an organization, for example, might not want to ask people about those conditions while the people were at work. For one thing, the workers couldn't be completely frank while their colleagues, and possibly their supervisor, could hear what they were saying. The workers might also feel the pressure to get back to work and give answers that they had not thought out carefully. It would be a better idea to interview people about their work conditions in a private setting away from the workplace.

Although we aren't professional researchers, we should show the same concern for the effects of context when we listen at work or at home. We can do this in two ways: (1) We can try to discover what influence the context may have had on what was said and (2) we can try to create a context in which listening can be more effective.

Interpreting Context   Trying to figure out what effect the context might have had on what was said is a little like playing a guessing game. You can't know for sure what the effect was. But it's important to try and to be aware what you heard might not have been the whole story. To analyze the effect that the context may have had on what was said, you can ask yourself a series of questions about the situation:

> Did the place affect what was said?
>> Was it private or could people overhear?
>> Was it comfortable or not?
>> Were there distractions?

Did the time of day affect what was said?
　　Was anyone tired, hungry, preoccupied?
　　Was anyone in a hurry to get somewhere else?

Did the other people present affect what was said?
　　Did the speakers have something to gain by what they said?
　　Did the speakers have something to lose by what they said?
　　Could anyone present have rewarded or punished the speakers for what
　　they said?

Did the occasion affect what was said?
　　Were there social rules about what could be said?
　　What else was going on that could affect what was said?

The context affects not only what other people will tell you, but also what you are able to understand. Distractions in the physical surroundings can prevent you from listening effectively. Noise in the room or distractions of people coming and going can interfere with listening. If it's too hot or too cold or if someone is smoking a cigar, sometimes all you can think about is getting out of there. At home you probably know you can't expect a family member to listen to you when they are involved in a task or when they are tired or distracted. If you're honest you may remember times when you didn't listen to your friends or family because you were worried about something or because your favorite TV show was on and you didn't want to be bothered. Unless you consciously put away other thoughts, you can't concentrate on listening.

Good listeners take advantage of a favorable situation to find out what they want to know. A few years ago a government agency was having a good deal of trouble because the press was getting inside information about programs before some members of the agency received that information. An investigation disclosed that the information was being gathered by reporters in the agency cafeteria. In the cafeteria employees gossiped freely about their work, and they were willing to share information with people who would listen to their problems. Reporters listened carefully and printed the information before it became official policy. The reporters took advantage of favorable context to do their job.

The context affects both what people will say and what it's possible to listen to and understand. By being aware of the effect that context has on the communication process, you can become a more successful listener.

I once had a job working in a nursing home. When I first started I thought some of the people there were just awful. They made jokes about the patients and were very grumpy and sharp sometimes. After I had worked there a while I figured out that they were grumpy because they had so much work to do. They didn't mean to be bad tempered; they were just in such a hurry. And they made the jokes to keep from caring too much. It's very difficult to work with sick people all day, especially when all of them don't get better. After a while I got to making jokes, too. It wasn't like I thought it would be.

Controlling the Effects of Context   The second way to take context into account when you listen is to analyze what effect the context might have on what people can say and try to create the context that would facilitate getting the kind of information you need or want. For example, one of the most difficult problems of communication in organizations is getting information from the workers to the managers. Although it's absolutely necessary for managers to know what is going on, managers are often the last to know when something goes wrong. This problem was one of the big issues in the *Challenger* space shuttle disaster of 1986 when the misgivings of the engineers were not reported to the people who made the decision to launch the shuttle. Sometimes workers don't talk to managers because they think managers don't care. Sometimes they fear punishment for something that was done wrong. Whatever the reason, it's in the manager's best interest to create a context in which it's both safe and desirable for workers to provide important information about what's going on in the work situation.

To the extent that you can control the context of communication, you can become a more effective listener. It's probably simplest to control the physical surroundings to get rid of unnecessary distractions and to create a place in which the person you're listening to will be comfortable to talk. By controlling the situation and not reacting impulsively, you can encourage people to tell you things they might otherwise hesitate telling you. If workers discover they will not be punished for bringing problems to the attention of supervisors, they will be more willing to provide negative information. And problem situations may be headed off before they develop. If you want your family or friends to talk to you about their personal concerns, you have to be a sympathetic listener. You may have to listen when you don't feel like listening; you may have to seek out or create opportunities to listen.

To create a good atmosphere in which to listen, you have to ask yourself many of the same questions you asked before:

How might the place affect what will be said?
   Will the place allow for privacy?
   Will the people be comfortable?
   What distractions might affect the listeners?
(What changes could you make to improve the place?)

Will the time of day affect how well people can listen?
   Will people be tired, hungry, preoccupied?
   Will anyone be in a hurry to get somewhere else?
(Would changing the time make a difference?)

How will the social occasion affect what is said?
   Are there social rules about what can be said?
(Is there any way to redefine the situation?)

Conferences and conventions are often places where listening is the prime activity, yet where physical and psychological conditions interfere with successful listening. If people have traveled some distance to the meeting, it seems a shame to waste any of the time, and meetings are often scheduled from early morning into the evening. Conferees suffering from the fatigue of a long journey are expected to sit quietly on hard chairs and pay attention to presentations lasting as long as two or three hours. These are hardly optimum conditions for successful listening.

For instance, people at meetings like to talk to their friends whom they may only see at such occasions. Unless sufficient time is left for participants to talk to one another informally, they may take meeting time to discuss their personal relationships. The purpose for the meeting may not be achieved if the participants are not attending to business when business should be the shared goal.

Another pitfall that conventions and conferences can fall into is the game of "one up." If conference members concentrate on trying to impress one another instead of sharing ideas and information, the result may be everybody showing off and nobody listening.

It's possible to avoid these problems by planning meetings so that participants can have plenty of time to refresh themselves and meet and greet their friends. Planning programs where everyone participates rather than having a series of formal presentations may help set an atmosphere of sharing instead of an atmosphere of competition. Careful planning with attention to the effects of the physical and social context can help create a positive atmosphere that encourages effective listening.

The same careful planning can be applied to personal relationships. If you want to say something important to a friend, you should be careful about the time and place you choose to say it. Imagine, for example, that you had a roommate who had personal habits that bothered you. Maybe the roommate was a "neatnik" who always had to have things just so: glasses polished and set in careful rows in the cupboard and the toilet paper roll put on in the right direction. When you felt that you couldn't stand any more, you might be tempted to lash out and shout and stamp around to vent your feelings. But how would you react if someone treated you that way?

Instead, it would be a better idea to give some thought to creating a situation in which you could sit down and discuss the topic rationally. Choose a time when neither of you is tired or busy and plan a way to bring up the topic that would not lead to defensiveness and argument. Looking for alternatives rather than delivering ultimatums would define a situation in which a compromise was possible.

When my wife and I were having problems with our marriage, the counselor helped us understand that we couldn't escape the rigid roles of what we thought husbands and wives should do. He suggested we do some talking in a place where we didn't have to be "husband" and "wife." So we went to the local Burger King and had a great fight. It was better than a soap opera and we laugh about it now. Changing the situation helped us break out of our roles.

LISTENING TO FEELINGS

We have probably all had the experience of saying something in anger or haste and having had to apologize or "take it back." We can most likely remember a time when we became enthusiastic about something before it happened and made rash promises that we couldn't keep later. Emotions affect our thinking and consequently often what we say. Good listeners take emotions as well as context into account when they interpret what they hear. Good listeners know that emotions can affect what they hear in two ways: (1) Emotion will affect what other people will say and (2) emotion will affect what we as listeners are willing or able to listen to.

Emotions Affect Communication

Jealousy, envy, anger, pride, admiration, love, or hate can color what people will say and often change the meaning of the words they utter. For centuries we have accepted Shakespeare's description of Richard III of England as a deformed, malevolent, despicable villain who viciously murdered his two small nephews in the Tower of London to preserve his own claim to the throne of England. The power of Shakespeare's poetry has disguised the fact that he was writing to please Elizabeth I, whose grandfather was the same Henry VII who killed Richard and usurped the throne for himself. It would not be likely that Elizabeth or the English people would accept a sympathetic treatment of Richard; to do so would be to throw doubt on the legitimacy of their current monarch's right to govern.

History is full of such stories. We believe them, not because of their inherent or documented truth, but because we need to believe them. The Puritans, we were taught in grade school, emigrated to the New World to escape religious persecution. In America they established a new society that was tolerant of other religious beliefs. Was that the whole story? Or even the real story? Religious persecution didn't serve to drive the Jews out of Warsaw and Nuremberg; instead, persecution served to bind them closer together in their ghettos. It took the Holocaust to clear those cities of their Jewish inhabitants. There is no reason to believe that religious persecution would necessarily affect the Puritans differently.

A different reading of history tells us that the Puritans left England expecting that nation to be destroyed by God for its evil practices, and they came to the New World to establish a perfect society on earth, ruled by God's laws. There is no room for religious dissent in a society ruled by God's laws (as interpreted, of course, by the Puritans). Dissenters were turned out into the wilderness. Because we believe strongly in religious tolerance as a principle of behavior, we are inclined to modify the stories of our founders to accord with our belief system. We let our feelings guide what we say and what we are willing or able to listen to.

One area where we specifically recognize the effect of desires and feelings on speech is in the field of politics. We know that in order to be elected to office many politicians tell the voters what they want to hear. When we listen to the speeches of political candidates we try to separate the "election rhetoric" from what candidates really stand for and are likely to carry out if they are elected.

We also acknowledge that some salespeople let their desire to make a sale affect the veracity of the claims they make for their products. We may even acknowledge that some of our acquaintances or friends have biases that affect their interpretation of particular situations or issues. Uncle Henry would always vote for the Democratic candidate in any election, and Aunt Martha never has a kind word for any of her husband's family. Bill will not hear a word in dispraise of his favorite hockey team, no matter what their record that year. When we listen to people who we know are biased, we take that bias into account. And we are all biased in some ways.

To a greater or lesser degree we may be aware of our personal biases, although it's more difficult to consider them when we listen. While it may be perfectly clear to us that Bill is prejudiced in his defense of his favorite team, Bill himself may not call his feelings "prejudice." Bill is being "loyal" to his team. Our own feelings, our "loyalties," may prevent us from listening to statements that are contrary to what we want or need to believe. This is a perfectly natural kind of behavior, but it can be dangerous in some circumstances.

Although we may concede that emotion is an important force in our private lives, we may not concede or recognize the role of emotion in our professional lives. The organizations we work for are supposed to be run on rational principles, unaffected by personal preference or passion. But, in fact, emotion is often an important element of the decisions made in governments and in business. And the person who's unaware of the existence of personal feuds, vendettas, and machinations in the work situation may fall victim to them unawares.

> Once I had a job as an interviewer for a communication audit. While I was interviewing this man about his work, he began telling me slanderous rumors about a woman in the organization. Well, I knew the woman and I knew what he was saying was slander, but I couldn't figure out why he was saying those things. Later I asked the woman herself, and she revealed that she and this man had been competitors for the job she now held. He had lost. To save his own face, he had begun a campaign of rumors to discredit her. Heaven knows how many people believed him!

Interpreting Nonverbal Communication

We rely largely on nonverbal information to determine what other people's feelings are. *Nonverbal communication* includes cues that aren't carried in the words people say, but rather, in the way the words are said and the actions we see. *Paralanguage* includes those voice qualities that aren't associated with the words themselves: pitch, rate, quality. Appearance and facial expressions are also important nonverbal cues to emotion. In addition, the way people use space and how they react to one another by looking or touching are also clues to the meaning of what they say.

We learn to interpret these nonverbal communication cues informally; that is, we are seldom taught nonverbal communication formally in school. We tend, therefore, not to think about how we interpret it or do it, but to assume that we are just behaving naturally when we decide, for example, whether someone is upset or lying to us. Explaining just how we came to the conclusion that the person we were talking to was angry or nervous would be a difficult task. By becoming more aware of how we make judgments about people's feelings and intentions, we can become better listeners.

It's very important to remember that interpretation of nonverbal communication is very closely tied to cultural norms; what's perceived as a highly emotional speech to someone from one culture may be interpreted differently by someone from another culture. For example, a person who speaks very quickly and uses dramatic inflections will usually be interpreted by Anglo-Americans as being very excited; but that's the normal style of speech for a Spanish-speaking person. Spanish speakers may interpret the slow speech and lack of inflection of a Scandinavian to be dullness or the lack of interest. In either case, what's being observed is in reality only differences in cultural norms. Interpretation of emotional cues is a very complex art, and one that should be practiced with great care.

Paralanguage   A lot of information is carried by the voice itself, those aspects of the voice that aren't connected with the words being said. If you know someone well, you can tell by the sound of his voice (even over the telephone) whether he is tired, ill, or upset. The pitch of a voice—high or low—can be interpreted to reveal emotion. We usually associate a rise in pitch with either excitement or nervousness. Inflection, the variation between high and low pitch, is another indicator of emotion. We may think that someone who speaks in a monotone is bored or ill. The rate at which a person speaks is another indicator of feelings; we seem to feel that people who speak quickly are more interested or involved than those who speak more slowly. Finally the quality of the voice—whether it's smooth or raspy, high pitched or deep, breathy or nasal—may also be interpreted as an indicator of the character or personality of the speaker. As listeners we should be aware that many of the judgments we make about the emotional state of the speaker come from our interpretation of nonverbal paralinguistic features of the speaker's voice.

Appearance   We also make judgments about what people actually mean, as opposed to what they say, by looking at them. We notice their appearance, their dress, their facial expressions. Again, if you know someone well, you can often tell by looking at her how she's feeling. We depend on facial expression as cues to whether or not someone is interested in what he is saying, whether someone cares if we understand, whether someone is telling the truth. If the expression on someone's face contradicts the words that person is saying, we generally conclude that the person is lying. We put more faith in the nonverbal communication cues than in the speech itself. Facial expression, then, is another important indicator of people's feelings.

> The people in my family never talk much about their feelings and they don't give much away by their expressions either. I guess you could call us poker faces. Sometimes that quality gets me in trouble in my classes, because teachers think I'm not interested because I don't react to what they're saying. But I'm really interested; I just don't show it much.

Space   Finally the way people use space and the way they orient themselves to others tell us other important facts about those people. Researchers studying people's use of space have looked at the use of space in several ways. Space is used as a measure of status, for example. A larger home or office usually means higher status. In an organization, the person with the large desk in the corner office is the most important person. Higher is also higher status, so the penthouse apartment costs more than apartments lower in the building.

On a more personal level, researchers have noticed that people claim differing amounts of personal space around themselves. Friends will usually sit or stand closer together when they talk than will acquaintances. We feel uncomfortable when strangers approach too closely. The amount of space people require around themselves differs from culture to culture, so what's acceptable as personal space to people from one country will not be acceptable to people from another country. In general, Americans and northern Europeans claim more personal space than do southern Europeans and people from Latin America.

Touching   Looking and touching are also forms of nonverbal communication that vary from culture to culture. In the United States it's customary for two people having a conversation to look directly into one another's eyes. In fact, it's impolite not to. But in other cultures, it's impolite to look directly at someone who's talking to you. Whatever the norms of the culture, breaking those norms is usually interpreted as poor manners or unfriendly behavior.

Good listeners must be aware that interpretations of nonverbal behavior provide them with most of their information about other people's emotions or attitudes. And that interpretation of nonverbal communication is very closely linked to cultural norms. We seldom question our assumptions about what nonverbal cues mean, although we should be very careful about making assumptions about such ambiguous cues. By examining our perceptions of other people's attitudes and feelings we can become more aware of the interpretations we have made and hopefully make fewer such mistakes.

> One time we invited our German friends over to watch the soccer matches on television with us. Some other friends of ours were there and we were all relaxing; one of the guys had his hands in his pockets. The German couple frowned at him, and the wife remarked, "He is very impolite." We learned that in Germany, you don't put your hands in your pockets.

Understanding Our Own Bias

Good listeners also have to search their own emotions to figure out to what extent what they heard was the result of their own attitudes and feelings toward either the speaker or the topic. An awareness of our own attitudes and biases can prevent us from misinterpreting what we hear and misunderstanding what others are saying. We can be affected by our feelings when we listen in two ways: (1) being self-centered in our listening and (2) responding emotionally when we listen.

Being Self-Centered   Being self-centered when we listen means that we don't recognize that the person who's talking may have a different frame of reference than we. We can make two important mistakes by being self-centered in our listening: We can fail to understand what we hear and we can fail to understand that the speaker may have a valid point of view that's nonetheless different from ours. In either case we deprive ourselves of important information and of the opportunity to see the world in a new way and to expand our knowledge of the world.

People who only listen to what they are already interested in fail to become interested in new ideas. Such people may demand that what they listen to have some clear relevance to their present purposes before they will bother to listen. They are limiting themselves to one set of topics and aren't searching out new topics to learn about. Consequently, when the world changes they aren't ready to change with it. Or when new opportunities arise they will not be ready for those opportunities. These are the students who continue to write with pencils on yellow pads while their classmates have mastered word processing. They are also people who have never heard of Ceylon or Bangladesh and are astonished when conflict or disaster in those distant parts of the world affects their own lives.

> I think my music appreciation class is the dumbest class I ever took. Yesterday, for example, we listened to German songs about an Elf King—for 50 whole minutes. I don't see how learning German lieder is going to help me get a job. It's a waste of my time!

Another way people can be self-centered when they listen is to fail to recognize that other people have different, but equally valid, points of view about what's important in the world. By only listening to and associating with the people who share our own attitudes, values, and beliefs, we insulate ourselves from the rest of the world. The danger is that the world will force itself into our consciousness in unpleasant or violent ways. This is what has been happening in South Africa, where the white minority is being forced by black protest and world opinion to consider the possibility that black people are human beings entitled to equal political rights and responsibilities. The notion is a novel one to some of the whites, and one with which they are ill-equipped to deal.

But this sort of blindness isn't limited to South Africa. It also occurs in our own lives. There are only 24 hours in a day and we are limited to being in one place at any one time. Therefore, we are all limited in our range of personal experiences and in the number of ideas to which we have been exposed by both geography and time. If we accept our limitations without questioning them we can fail to be prepared when people with different experiences and values demand the right to be heard and the right to shape the world in which they live.

> I'm giving a speech on Martin Luther King and his work for voter registration in the South. But I'm having a problem with the speech. Most of my audience wasn't born when the civil rights movement was strong in the 1960s and besides they are white. Why should they care that blacks in the South couldn't vote in the 1950s?

To be good listeners we need to remember that there are many different kinds of people with many different experiences, attitudes, values, and beliefs. There isn't just one right way to be or to think. By recognizing that other people have had different kinds of experiences and that those experiences have led them to different beliefs and values, we may be able to learn something new about the world. Movies and television have brought us stories about people from remote parts of the world. Increased immigration from Third World countries and from Latin America is bringing us in daily contact with people whose ethnic backgrounds are quite different from mainstream America. In order to deal with this changing world we should be able to put aside our own ideas long enough to give other ideas a fair hearing. We must avoid being self-centered in order to listen with understanding.

Responding Emotionally   It's often hard to listen to someone who disagrees with us without getting upset. It's very easy to become angry and to try to set the other person straight, usually without hearing them out. Emotional reactions serve to mobilize our bodies for action; they raise our hormone levels and cause our muscles to tense and our nerves to respond quickly. When you're nervous, you just can't sit still, and when you're angry you have to act your anger out in some way, by either talking or acting violently. By reacting emotionally—getting impatient or angry—you effectively stop communication and deprive yourself of the opportunity to learn. It's important, therefore, to learn to control your emotional reactions until the other person has finished what he was saying.

If you can learn not to react until the other person has completed his thoughts, then there are two possible outcomes. First, you may discover that you weren't, in fact, disagreeing about issues but only about words. You may have been the bystander at such a disagreement between two of your friends or two members of your family. They were arguing away, when you could see that they were actually on the same side of the fence. It may have taken some time to get them to calm down and see that they actually didn't disagree as much as they thought they did.

> I can remember when my brother and my mom used to go around and around, fighting like cats and dogs. He knew just what to say to make her mad, and then she would start yelling. Then they would both be yelling at each other and nobody would be listening. It would end up with him stomping out and her being so mad we couldn't talk to her the rest of the day. I knew they both cared about each other, but they just kept fighting because nobody was listening. Sometimes it seemed like they both tried to misunderstand what the other one was saying.

The other possible outcome of hearing someone else out is that you still disagree when you are finished listening. In that case you may be justified in your emotional reaction. But when you speak or act you will be assured that you're acting on the basis of knowledge and you will be prepared for the consequences. By understanding what the other person is saying, you may find some way to convince her to rethink her position. Or, if it's hopeless, you may decide that it isn't worth the effort to argue with her. Whatever the outcome, you will certainly come away from the situation with more knowledge than you had before—the outcome of listening successfully for information.

LISTENING FOR PATTERNS AND IDEAS

Undoubtedly you have at one time or another had to listen to someone give directions that were so mixed up you couldn't understand what the person was saying. Maybe you were asking for directions to find a place that you had never been to before or for directions to do some complex task, like operating a piece of equipment. More likely you had to listen to a lecturer in school whose explanations were so disorganized that they didn't make any sense. Unless you could recognize a pattern to what they were saying, you couldn't understand what they meant. Finding the organizational pattern is crucial to understanding what you are listening for. To find the organizational pattern, you need to listen for main ideas and transitions, words that indicate the connections between ideas.

Organizational Patterns

Fortunately for us, there are a limited number of common organizational patterns that we use over and over again. These *organizational patterns* represent our natural ways of thinking and reasoning about the world. There are seven of these organizational patterns: time, space, categories, analogy, contrast, relationship, and problem solution. If you can identify what pattern the speaker is using, you will be a much more effective listener. If there is no organizational pattern, it may be impossible to understand the speaker's message.

Time Pattern   One of the most common forms of talk is telling stories, and the organization of story form is called time pattern. In the world around us things take shape, grow and develop, and wither or die. So stories about the world take the shape of beginning, middle, and end. We can organize our experience into historical time, by telling how something happened, or process time, by telling how to do something. In either case the structure of the pattern is the same, as shown in Figure 4.1.

    If you determine that the speaker is using time as the organizational pattern, you can predict what will come next and understand what's being said. Maybe someone is explaining a problem he has. If he tells you how things got that way,

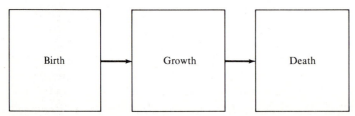

Figure 4.1 Historical time.

he will probably use time pattern. Or, if someone is telling you what she plans to do in the future, that would also be a time pattern.

The transitions that will indicate you're listening to a time pattern are words like "first," "second," "next," and "finally." If the pattern is historical time, you may hear words like "at first," "very early," "later," or "at last." These are the words we use to connect things in time.

Space Pattern   Another common task in communication is describing something. In order to describe anything, we usually identify the important parts that go together to make up the whole. The pattern for that kind of talk is called space pattern, and there are two kinds of space patterns. The first space pattern describes something that exists in real space, sometimes called a map. Describing a place or a machine, or a physical system like a heating or cooling plant would require the use of a map space pattern. Sometimes it's even easier to draw a picture than to describe things in words. Often diagrams accompany messages that are formulated in a space pattern.

The second kind of space pattern is most commonly used to describe organizations that don't exist in real space but that must have particular parts in relation to one another in order to function. Organization charts for corporations or governmental bodies are the most common form of this pattern, called a figurative space pattern. The organization pattern of the United Nations, for example, looks like the diagram in Figure 4.2.

The diagram illustrates that the General Assembly is the central body served by five other groups that have separate functions: Security Council, International Court of Justice, Secretariat, Economic and Social Council, and Trusteeship Council. A space pattern, then, explains how things are made or how they work by explaining the relationship of the parts to the whole.

Some transitions that may indicate you're listening to a space pattern would be "one important part," "another component," "connecting these," "working together," and so on. Some other words you might listen for are "is made up of," "comprise the whole," and "is related to." You can probably think of other examples.

Category Patterns   Very often we talk about different kinds or types of things. For example, there are several kinds of insurance: home insurance, liability insurance, medical insurance, auto insurance, and so on. Or we might say there are several kinds of governments: parliamentary governments, representative governments, monarchies, and so on. Whenever we break things down into various types we are using category patterns.

This pattern differs from the space pattern, in that there is no necessary way to designate different kinds or types of a thing, while the parts of a whole are necessary divisions. To illustrate the differences, we might take the topic "schools." We could use a space pattern to explain that schools are composed of administrators, teachers, students, and service personnel. You can't run a school without these people. But schools can be categorized in a number of different ways. For example, we can categorize schools by how they are financed: There

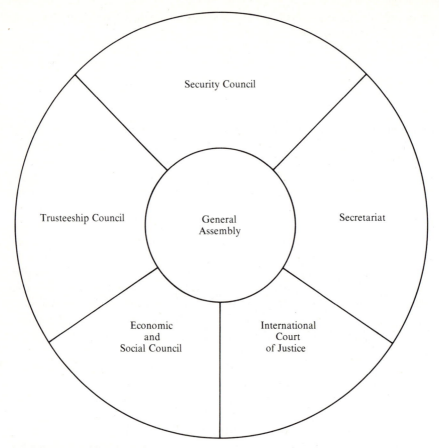

Figure 4.2 Figurative space.

are public, private, and parochial schools. Or we can categorize schools by the ages of the people who attend them: There are elementary, secondary, and post-secondary schools. And then there are various types of postsecondary schools by their subject matter: colleges, trade schools, and so on. The category scheme the speaker chooses depends on what point is being made. (See Figure 4.3.)

If you notice that someone is talking about types of things or ways of doing things, you can be sure that the person is using the category pattern of organization. This is undoubtedly the most common organizational pattern. Words commonly used to connect categories of things are "another type," "another way to," "a third style," and so on.

Analogy Pattern We often talk about how things are like one another. Messages organized by comparing two things that are alike are organized into an analogy pattern. This organization pattern is often used to compare familiar things (foot-

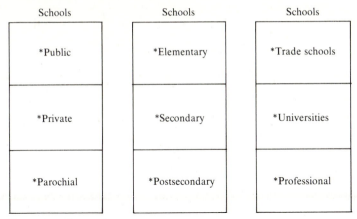

Figure 4.3 Categories.

ball) with unfamiliar things (rugby). Or it can be used to show how something is good by comparing a particular object with the standards for judging that object. The Boston fern makes a good houseplant because it needs only moderate light, thrives at room temperature, and tolerates variations in humidity. As listeners, once we understand that two objects are being compared, it's pretty easy to understand what's being said. (See Figure 4.4.)

As you might predict, transitions used between ideas that are like one another include words such as "like," "closely resembling," "in the same manner," "along the same lines," and the like.

Contrast Pattern   The opposite of analogy pattern is, of course, contrast pattern—telling how two things are different from one another. Contrast patterns are used in the same way as analogy patterns—to show how two familiar things are actually different or to show how some object doesn't meet the standards for a good object. An orchid isn't a good houseplant for someone without a green-

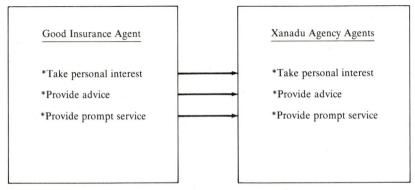

Figure 4.4 Analogy.

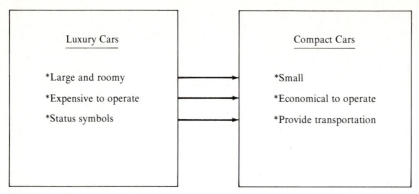

Figure 4.5 Contrast.

house, because orchids need a very specific range of temperatures and carefully controlled amounts of light and humidity to thrive. Or you might show how men's and women's volleyball differ, although they might look the same to an uneducated bystander. Contrast is also a common and simple pattern of organization for messages. (See Figure 4.5.)

Transitions that connect different things might include "on the contrary," "unlike the previous," "in sharp contrast," "very different," or "contrary to expectations."

Relationship Pattern In order to understand our environment, we have to understand how various things are related to one another. If we raise taxes, what will happen to individuals and businesses? If we take a prescription drug, what side effects can occur? What's the effect if we send three-year-olds to nursery school? Is there any relationship between children's early upbringing and their performance in school? These kinds of questions are formulated into a pattern we call relationship pattern.

We usually express relationships in terms of cause and effect, although there are other ways of expressing relationships. Sometimes things vary inversely. For

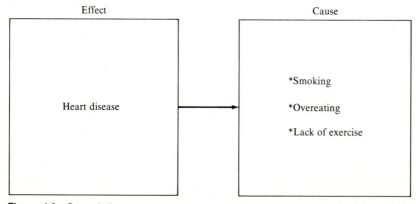

Figure 4.6 Cause/effect.

example, since states have raised the drinking age from 18 to 21, the number of traffic accidents resulting in fatalities have decreased dramatically. Whenever two things covary, we can use their relationship as an organizing pattern to talk about them. Relationship pattern is one that we commonly look for when people are talking about politics, business, or health. (See Figure 4.6.)

Sometimes messages start with effects and then move to the causes; sometimes messages start with the causes and move to effects. In either case, once you understand that the message is about the relationship between two things, you can understand what's being said.

Words that indicate relationships are the focus of attention might include "closely related," "consequently," "following from this," "cause the following," "are influenced by," and so on.

Problem-Solution Relationship   Whenever people want to change something, they have to explain why and how. To do that they generally use a pattern called a problem-solution pattern. This is a formal pattern, governed by rules of logic. The message must begin with a description of the problem, often in terms of a cause and effect. The description of the problem will probably detail what bad consequences result from the problem situation, whom they affect, and what the cost of not correcting the problem will be. Then the message will detail the solution, and explain how that solution will deal with the problem. The good consequences of implementing the solution will also be explained. (See Figure 4.7.)

Some words to help you recognize problem-solution patterns are, of course, "problem" and "solution." There are also such phrases as "to remedy," "to prevent," and "to solve."

Word Meanings

Once you have identified the organizational pattern of a message, you can grasp the structure of the idea that you are listening for. But in order to understand

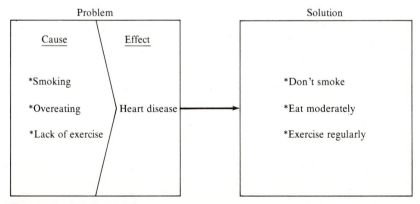

Figure 4.7   Problem solution.

that idea completely, you will also have to be able to understand the language in which the idea is phrased.

One of the important problems of listening to understand is the problem of shared vocabulary. If you don't understand the words someone is using, then you will not be able to understand what they are talking about. The question of identifying what someone is talking about is often most difficult in the context of work, especially if you're in a new situation or learning a new job. Each type of work seems to have its special vocabulary, its lingo known to insiders, that you have to learn in order to be able to function.

> "Hey, Judy, I can't remember how to pctrans this file up to the mainframe. What's the procedure?"
>
> "Well, first you have to get it out of ASCII. You can do that by printing to disk. Then you use the pctrans up command with the diskdrive and filename followed by the CMS filename. Got it?"
>
> "No, come here and show me."

The problem of acquiring a technical vocabulary doesn't only apply to using machines. Any job has a technical vocabulary that you have to master to be competent. If you have been through school you have learned the educational jargon of instructional objectives, behavior modification, positive reinforcement, and constructive criticism. Just getting a bank account can be enough to give you a headache; you have to choose among so many different kinds. Whenever you meet a new situation, you may face the problem of learning how to understand and express yourself in a new vocabulary.

Another problem in listening to understand is related to the problem of vocabulary, but it's more subtle than just sharing words in common. This problem is one of shared experience. Often people who use the same words have very different experiences of those words. In English class you learned that words have both denotation—the actual thing the word refers to—and connotation—the feelings attached to a word. For example, the word "school" can denote nursery school, elementary school, high school, technical school, college, graduate school, professional school, or military school. While it's fairly simple to discover which kind of school someone is referring to, it's the connotations that can get you in trouble. Two people with different experiences of school may think they understand one another, while in fact they are worlds apart. An individual's experience with school may have been positive or negative. Someone who's not sensitive to connotations can easily misunderstand what's being said and respond inappropriately.

> My friend's mother was saying that she thought the best time of her life was when she was in high school. Can you imagine? I thought she was nuts. All I can remember of high school was following dumb rules. You would get in trouble if you were two minutes late to a class; they expected you to get from class to class in less than five minutes. If you had to go to the bathroom, forget it! I hated high school. Finally I figured out she was talking about the proms and

basketball games. At our school we never had a winning team, so nobody went to the games. I don't know, it must be real strange to think the best time of your life was over before you were 20. And you spent it in school!

Listening to understand involves listening for the pattern of ideas when we hear a message and listening to understand the words the speaker is using. By looking for the common organizational patterns, you can make the task easier. And by remembering to check that your understanding of important words and ideas are the same as those of the speaker, you can avoid much misunderstanding.

INTERPRETING SILENCE

More than one social scientist (Bateson, 1972; Sapir, 1949) has remarked that silence is often as eloquent as speech, that in fact "You can't not communicate." That observation refers to the idea that whenever two people are together, each of them interprets what the other is doing. If you're sitting in a waiting room with a stranger who refuses to look at you or speak to you, you "get the message" that that person wants to be left alone. You have interpreted the lack of behavior as meaning. So, in a very real sense, you can't not communicate because anything you do (or don't do) will be interpreted by another person as meaningful.

As listeners we must interpret silence as well as speech, but the problem with silence is that it's ambiguous. It never has a specific meaning; the meaning of silence always depends on what else is going on. We interpret silence within the context of the interaction, and two different people often make two different interpretations of the same silence. Researchers who study silence even have a difficult time defining what constitutes silence and what doesn't. How long, for example, does someone have to pause before speaking before that pause becomes "silence"? Half a second? A second? Five seconds? Or, if we look at pauses between statements as silence, how do we classify pauses that are filled with sounds like "umm," "ahhh," or "well"? The answer to these kinds of questions seems to be "it depends," so in this section we will confine ourselves to illustrating some of the different ways silence can be interpreted. It's up to you as a listener to be aware that your interpretation of silence may not be the same as that of the nonspeaker.

Positive or Negative Silence

For one thing, silence can be seen as negative—the absence of speaking—or positive—no need for words. If you expect someone to write you a letter or call, and you don't get a letter or phone call, you might interpret that silence as negative. You didn't get what you expected. You might begin to wonder whether the person is ill or angry. If someone you know doesn't speak to you, you may feel you were snubbed. Silence can be unfriendly. It can convey hostility and anger, as when former friends are no longer on speaking terms.

On the other hand, silence can be both friendly and comforting if it conveys unspoken understanding or sympathy. Friends who know one another very well often feel they don't need to speak. When you feel pain or sorrow, the silent presence of a friend may be more comforting than speech from someone you don't know well or don't like. Silence may be interpreted as respect—not interrupting what someone else is doing or not speaking until spoken to.

The interpretation of silence as negative or positive communication depends on whether or not silence is seen as appropriate in the situation. If you're expecting speech, silence will be interpreted as negative. Silence that seems appropriate will often be interpreted as positive. It's clear, then, that two people can have different interpretations of the same silence. Or the same person can interpret silence differently in different situations. Walker (1985) reported that while lawyers advised their own clients to think before they spoke, the same lawyers interpreted pauses made by other lawyers' clients as evidence of lying. Other researchers have discovered that the interpretation of silence as negative or positive may depend on your ethnic group. Tannen (1985) reported that Italians, Italian-Americans, Afro-Americans, and New York Jews often interpret silence as the absence of communication, hence a negative, impolite behavior to be avoided. Other groups like Finns and American Indians look on silence as positive communication—the absence of noise.

Purposes for Silence

Silence serves different purposes in different situations. Silence serves as the background against which we measure talk. In this sense, pausing is a device to mark the changes between speakers in a conversation. When one speaker pauses long enough, it's time for the other person to speak. If you pause long enough, the other person finally feels obliged to fill the silence with talk. This social rule is often used by counselors and psychologists to encourage their clients to speak.

Social Silence   Silence is also a part of the system of social rules that marks status and polite behavior. People who are new to groups aren't expected to do much talking; established members talk. Younger people are often silent in the presence of older people as a sign of respect. In an executive meeting, everyone waits for the president to speak first. Talking out of turn or talking at the wrong time is considered impolite, if not downright disrespectful. There are times when social rules call for everyone to be silent, as in church or at ceremonies. These formal occasions have specific rules for when people talk and when they don't; who speaks and who is silent. So silence is an important part of the social rules for communicative behavior.

Emotional Silence   Silence can also serve as an indication of emotional state. If a person who's naturally talkative becomes silent, you may well infer that that person is upset about something. People who are angry with one another frequently resort to "not speaking" as an indication of their feelings. Silence is a defense against the undue exercise of power; silence can serve a defiance against authority. "You can't make me tell," might be a correct interpretation of silence sometimes. And people can use silence to cut off communication, figuratively if not literally turning their faces to the wall.

Symbolic Silence   Finally silence can even carry symbolic meaning in certain situations. Imagine that someone you know has asked you to do a favor that you're really not willing to do. One way of avoiding a direct refusal is to ignore the request and change the subject. Silence in that case carries the meaning "No." In some other situations, silence may mean "yes." In the traditional wedding ceremony when the pastor asks if anyone knows any obstacles to the union of this woman and man, silence is interpreted as assent.

Silence, then, can serve many and varied purposes in communication and the meaning of a specific silence can vary with the context. The most important fact to remember about silence is that the meaning is almost always ambiguous—open to various interpretations. Before you react to silence, you should check to see whether your interpretation is the only possible one, or whether your reaction to the silence is appropriate.

SUMMARY

In this chapter we discussed four important factors we need to pay attention to when we listen to understand. The first factor was context. We need to understand that what people say and don't say and how they phrase their thoughts depend to a large extent on the situation and the listeners who are present. Another aspect of listening to understand involved understanding the feelings behind the words. We can and often do use words to hide things or to say things indirectly. By understanding what people are feeling we can better assess what they mean. A third part of listening to understand involved identifying the structural pattern of messages to identify the main points and the purpose of the message. We also need to understand that words are symbolic: They can mean different things to different people. Finally we need to interpret silence, which is an especially meaningful and ambiguous part of communication between people.

SUGGESTED ACTIVITIES

1. Collect cartoons, stories, and pictures that illustrate the importance of context on the meaning of communication. Share these with the class and see if you can find categories of context in which meanings are specific.

2. Take a simple phrase like "But I thought Jane and Philip were friends" and see how many different ways you can say it and how many different interpretations you can get from the single sentence. How might the context differ for these different interpretations?

3. Watch a soap opera or a situation comedy with the sound turned down. What emotions can you identify from the actors' expressions and gestures? Does the context affect how you interpret their feelings?

4. Listen to a radio drama or listen to a television drama without watching

the television. What cues are there to meaning in the voices of the people who are speaking?

5. Go to a public place like a bus terminal, a post office, or a bank. Notice how the space is arranged. What markers are there for "official business" and what markers for "outsiders"? How do people claim personal space in that setting?

6. As you listen to lectures, try to pick out the organizational patterns. What clues can you find to help you identify the patterns? Are some patterns more common than others? What are they? You can also look for organizational patterns in business speeches and presentations, sermons, and public service announcements of various kinds.

REFERENCES AND RECOMMENDED READING

Adler, Ron, and Neil Towne. *Looking Out/Looking In.* San Francisco: Holt, Rinehart and Winston, 1978.

Bateson, Gregory. *Steps to an Ecology of Mind.* New York: Ballantine, 1972.

Goffman, Erving. *The Presentation of Self in Everyday Life.* Garden City, NY: Doubleday, 1959.

Merabian, Albert. *Silent Messages.* Belmont, CA: Wadsworth, 1971.

Sapir, Edward. "Speech as a Personality Trait." In *Selected Writings of Edward Sapir in Language, Culture, and Personality,* edited by David Mandelbaum. Berkeley, CA: University of California Press, 1949.

Tannen, Deborah. "Silence: Anything But." In *Perspectives on Silence,* edited by Deborah Tannen and Muriel Saville-Troike. Norwood, NJ: Ablex, 1985.

Walker, Anne G. "Linguistic Manipulation, Power, and the Legal Setting." In *Power Through Discourse,* edited by Leah Kedar. Norwood, NJ: Ablex, 1985.

chapter 5

Listening to Maintain Relationships

When you finish this chapter you should be able to:

1. Describe the importances of relationships in our lives.
2. Distinguish between interactional relationships and transactional relationships.
3. Explain how to check reality in both kinds of relationships.
4. Distinguish between empathic listening and sympathetic listening.
5. Define dual perspective and explain two ways to take a dual perspective.
6. Describe three important communication principles and explain their relationship to listening skills.

When you finish this chapter you should be able to define these important concepts:

1. interaction
2. transaction
3. reality checking
4. norms
6. dual perspective
7. empathic listening
8. sympathetic listening
9. abstractions
10. operational definitions
11. mirror questions

Humans are social creatures. By nature people are more comfortable and happy when they are around other people. Solitary confinement is often used as a punishment, because it deprives people of a basic need for companionship and stimulation that is as necessary to them as are food and sleep. In order for people to exist in groups, however, they have to create and maintain relationships with one another. An important element of the creation and maintenance of relationships is the activity of listening.

Other animals besides humans have social natures. Many animals gather in herds or flocks for protection or comfort, or because it's easier to exist by cooperation than by competition. Bees, ants, and termites are called "social insects" because they exist in communities and take cooperative roles to maintain that community. But animals associate in groups that are determined by the families or communities into which they are born. Seldom do animals leave one herd or flock for another because they like the individuals in the other group better or because the rules of that group allow them more individual freedom. Humans, on the other hand, have unique opportunities to choose or create affiliations with other people. The fact that humans are reasoning animals means they can consciously create and maintain relationships they find most satisfactory to their particular values and needs. You can choose which schools to attend, which clubs to join, which companies to work for, and with which of your relatives to associate. You listen to decide who you will associate with and what groups you will belong to. And it's an important part of learning how to be effective in groups and intimate relationships.

Actually we are born into some relationships; we are born into a family and a community. But families change and move, and new family relationships are created by marriages. We also create and maintain relationships with new friends when we move or when we change jobs or when other aspects of our lives change. At work we make new relationships when we are promoted or change jobs or occupations. Statistical studies show that the average worker will hold four different jobs during his or her lifetime, and many people seem to be married that many times.

As social and personal situations change, people are often faced with the necessity of breaking old relationships and beginning new ones. This is often a difficult process, and one for which we have little formal training. There are no courses in school about "Meeting and Making New Friends" or "Ways to Leave Your Lover." There is considerable evidence that people are having trouble creating and maintaining satisfactory family and work relationships in the modern world. The divorce rate is at an all-time high, and new groups to serve the needs of lonely people are proliferating. In other words, a great deal of evidence exists that people are having increasing difficulty in their personal and professional relationships.

The creation and maintenance of all relationships depend largely on good communication. To the extent that people share goals, knowledge, interests, attitudes, emotions, and values, they build the bonds that create the groups in which they live. You can check this out for yourself by thinking about how you make new friends. Whenever you meet someone new, the first goal of conversation is almost always to find out what you share.

> "Where do you come from?" "Topeka? Oh, my aunt used to live there."
>
> "Where do you work?" "Amalgamated? Oh, I have a friend who is a financial analyst for that same company."
>
> "What kind of music do you like?" "Rusty Screwdriver? Oh, that's one of my favorite groups, too."

By listening to one another, you find out what you have in common and make a decision about whether you want to begin or continue a relationship.

We all create and maintain relationships on various levels throughout our lives. We have intimate relationships with family and lovers, social relationships with friends, professional relationships with colleagues and co-workers, and we exist in a larger community of clubs, churches, and other organizations. We all live in communities, towns or cities, states, and a nation. Each of these kinds of social relationships is important to our welfare and well-being, and each takes careful attention to create and maintain.

INTERACTIONAL AND TRANSACTIONAL RELATIONSHIPS

Some scholars of interpersonal communication—private communication between individuals—have identified two general kinds of relationships: interactions and transactions. *Interactions* are the public or formal kinds of relationships we carry on at work or in other clearly defined and more or less public situations. For instance, the doctor-patient relationship would be classified as an interaction, because the roles are clearly defined for each person. Doctors ask questions and give advice; patients answer questions and take advice. Similarly, the teacher-student relationship, the supervisor-employee relationship, and the clerk-customer relationship are clearly defined by social rules and custom. These relationships are called interactions.

More intimate relationships like those of lover-lover, friend-friend, child-parent, and wife-husband are not public and therefore are not clearly defined. These relationships—*transactions*—must be negotiated privately between the two people involved. Some models are available for these kinds of relationships as they are portrayed on television and in the movies and in books, but each intimate relationship is based on some set of private agreements about what's important and what's not important and how the two people will conduct themselves in relation to one another and to the world. We generally feel that the way two people conduct a private relationship is no one else's business. That's what makes it a private relationship.

In each of these kinds of relationships, listening plays a crucial role in determining what's expected of us as participants in the relationship and what's appropriate or valuable in the relationship. In interactional relationships we need to check reality to find out what the rules are. In transactional relationships we need to check reality to find out what the other person wants and expects from the relationship.

Reality Checking

Most of the public world in which we go about and do our business every day is regulated by rules of various kinds. Some are official rules and some are unofficial expectations. As we grow up we learn these rules, and we learn to behave in accordance with other people's expectations. Some of the rules are taught to us formally, but some of them we learn on our own by observing and imitating what people around us do.

The official rules are written down and called laws or regulations. We have federal, state, and local laws made by our legislatures. There are regulations for agencies like the post office or the police department. Companies have standard operating procedures that are written down. Other rules are spelled out in contracts, including loan agreements and insurance policies. You can find out these official rules by reading them.

But many of the important rules for behaving in public are never written down; everybody just knows them. Such rules are called *norms* by sociologists, who study the behavior of people in groups. Knowing the norms is a very important part of becoming an effective member of society and of being successful. But finding out what they are is a more complex process, because they are not written down anywhere, and because people aren't always aware that they are following norms. When people are following norms they often think they are just "behaving naturally." Whenever you see someone who's behaving "unnaturally," it's a pretty good bet that the person is breaking some of the unwritten rules for behavior.

> I have this habit of talking to myself when I'm alone. I tell myself what I have to do next or think out what I will say to someone in some situation. Once in a while I catch myself doing that in public—when I'm riding the bus or walking down the street. People look at me funny when I talk to myself, like they thought I was crazy or something.

Checking Reality in Interactions In interactions, *reality checking* refers to the action of finding out the norms or unwritten rules by which people operate in particular groups. Some reality checking is done by observing what other people are doing, and some reality checking is done by listening to what other people say about what they are doing and why they are doing it. A few examples will help to make the process clearer.

When you begin a new job, you will probably be told by the boss or supervisor what you are expected to do. The rules that you are told are only part of the knowledge you will need to be successful. You will also have to discover the informal rules or norms for the performance for your job. You can discover these informal rules by listening to the talk around you. For example, in most jobs there are provisions for "breaks" from your work. In some jobs those breaks are formally designated and occur at regularly scheduled and carefully timed intervals. In other jobs, you can "take a break" when you feel like it without incurring any punishment. If you don't discover and follow the unwritten rules, you can get in trouble.

> When I started working at the card store on Sundays I discovered we were scheduled to take a lunch break from 12:00 to 12:20, although we came to work at 11:00 and worked until 6:00. When I worked with Ellen, she stuck to that schedule. But when I worked with June, we took our lunch break later, about 2:00 or 2:30 when we really needed to rest. I also discovered that when I worked in the evening I could keep a Coke under the counter and drink it, but the "day ladies" wouldn't allow that. There were all kinds of funny rules and exceptions I had to learn to get along with everyone there.

In many jobs there are also unwritten rules about how much work you should get done in a given time. If you exceed that amount of work, you will hear remarks like: "Oh, Randy is trying to show us all up by being a hotshot" or "Hey there, what's your hurry? You trying to impress the supervisor or what?" These remarks are designed to point out the unwritten rules for the performance of your job. On the other hand, if your performance is not up to standard, you will also hear pointed remarks or start getting dirty looks from other employees. Listening for these kinds of remarks will reveal what the expectations for your performance are. You will be listening to check reality in the workplace.

Sometimes we check reality by stating our perceptions or feelings to other people to see if they see things the same way we do. Teachers who have a problem with a particular student may ask other teachers whether that student gives them problems, too. Students ask one another about teachers to see who's easy or hard, who's fair or unfair, or whatever else they want to know about the teacher. New parents check with their own parents and with friends who have children to see whether their babies are normal. By listening to other people's talk about their experiences, we can check our own understanding of the world around us.

> After I came home from the hospital with my new daughter, I felt so depressed. I thought I was crazy. After all, here was this new baby we had hoped and planned for, and now that she was here I was depressed? I called my friend who told me that my depression was common for a lot of new mothers. It even had a name: "postpartum blues." Well, I sure felt better about that. It was bad enough feeling depressed; I didn't want to think I was crazy.

As our lives change and we adopt or adapt to new roles, we often check our perceptions of those new roles with people who are "authorities." When you started high school, you watched the upper-class students carefully to find out how to behave like a high school student. By listening to them talk about classes, you learned what your attitudes toward classwork and studying should be. Perhaps you learned that certain people who talked to the teachers a lot were called "teacher's pets" or "brownnoses." Perhaps you learned that it was "cool" to stay up all night studying before an exam and to complain about how difficult the exam was (whether or not you found it difficult). You probably spent a lot of time on the phone or at local hangouts checking with your friends about what they were wearing and what music they were listening to and what they thought about the other kids and teachers at school. In high school it suddenly seemed very important to think the way all the other kids thought. The penalty for being different was to be called names—oddball or nerd or crazy—and not to be included in many activities.

> I remember going to a "slumber party" when I was a junior in high school. The girls stayed up all night, talked dirty, and smoked cigars. I thought that was boring, and I said so. I was never invited to another slumber party, which pleased me just as well. But I was also excluded from a lot of other parties, which didn't please me so well.

As you moved into adolescence you spent a lot of time learning how to think about and how to treat people of the opposite sex. Not much of what you learned was written down; you learned by watching and listening to the people around you. You probably got together with your friends and talked about the other sex and agreed on how to behave toward them. You learned what it meant to be "seeing" or "dating" or "going with" or "going steady with" or whatever other terms you used to indicate the various categories of relationships between the sexes in your group. Listening to what other people say about how to behave properly is called reality checking, and it's an important part of learning to play an accepted role in society.

There were always people who didn't learn the rules. These people were labeled "crazy," "stupid," or "nerds." Some people discovered the rules and chose not to follow them; other people just never seemed to catch on. Social researchers have discovered that the most popular people (including most leaders in groups) achieve their positions partly from carefully following the norms of the groups of which they are members. Then, after they achieve a high position in the group, they are rewarded by not having to follow the norms.

As you left high school and got a job or entered a profession, you discovered that there were rules for how to dress, how to talk, and how to behave in that profession. You also learned the accepted attitudes toward the various categories of people you worked with daily. People who work as clerks in stores don't have uniforms, but they all seem to dress alike. They also learn to behave like clerks, so that you can pick one out when you look. If you have ever been mistaken for a clerk in a store, you will remember how astonished you were and maybe a little insulted. Teachers behave like teachers, and after a few years they seem to take on some of the characteristics of their students. Have you ever noticed that you can tell a first-grade teacher from a seventh-grade teacher? Bank tellers are supposed to act like bank tellers. Each job or profession has its own ways of thinking and acting that you learn if you begin to work in that position.

We aren't advocating that you always follow whatever rules seem to be set down for the group of which you're a member. It's important, however, to know what the rules are for appropriate behavior in that group so you can make a conscious decision about whether or not you want to conform. Not knowing proper or appropriate behavior can prevent you from being an effective member of the group or can ensure that other people label you dumb or crazy. Knowing and choosing what norms you want to follow can help you be more effective.

> In the corporation I work for, the only way women get ahead is to sleep with the boss. Everybody knows it. We even joke about it. Fortunately I'm not looking for a position as supervisor or vice president. I don't know whether or not I'll stay with this corporation. I don't know whether it's better anywhere else. It's a real problem.

Finding out what the unwritten rules are is done by a process of inference. People will not always tell you what the rules are; sometimes they don't even know they are unconsciously following rules. You will only notice the rules when they are broken. One thing you can do is listen to what people say about people who are successful and rewarded by the group. Figure out what the winners are rewarded for. Are the people everyone respects people who get along with everyone? Or are they people who are very good at their jobs? What are the respected people doing that makes them valuable to the group?

Then look at the people who are criticized or made fun of in the group. What are they doing that's different from what the people who are rewarded are doing? What do people say about the "losers"? Do they look different or sound different from the rest of the group? What kinds of things do these people talk about? Do or don't they get along well with others? Are they sensitive to what others in the group are saying about them?

> I was a cheerleader in high school, and I didn't know I was following norms until I took a group discussion class. The teacher asked what the norms were for my group, and I sat down and figured them out. Some of them really surprised me. One norm was that cheerleaders couldn't be fat. I only realized that when I remembered how astonished we all were when a fat girl was chosen as a cheerleader one year. Another norm was that all the cheerleaders dated guys on the football team. It was just what everyone did.

If you decide that you want to be a valued member of a group, you must figure out what you can do to become valuable. You must watch what the valued members do and follow their lead. If you decide you don't care about the group, you can also make the decision not to conform to the group norms. But you should make a considered choice based on the knowledge of what the group rules are.

Checking Reality in Transactions   *Checking reality* in transactions is a process of finding out what the other person is thinking and feeling. Too often, we assume that other people feel the same way we do, assuming everyone is like us. Unfortunately that kind of attitude can cause us trouble, because people can have very different interpretations of the same situation. Even people who have grown up in the same family often differ from one another. Coordinating what you think with what someone else thinks or what you feel with what someone else feels is a delicate process of figuring out where you agree and where you differ. A few examples might make this difference clearer.

Imagine that you have a brother (if you don't have one) and imagine that your brother has permission to take the car out on Saturday night. But he has to be back by midnight. Then one night he doesn't come home until 3:00 A.M. Your parents stay up until he comes in. The minute he gets in your parents begin to get on his case and threaten never to let him have the car again. Your brother feels he had a good reason for being late (whatever his reason was—it's not important) and he thinks your parents are being unreasonable and nasty. You, on the other hand, were there listening to them worry about whether he had been in an accident, or whether the car had broken down. They imagined him in the emergency room or in the police station or stranded on a dark road. You know they are really very relieved that your brother is home safely, but they are letting off steam by scolding him. They are really scolding him for frightening them, but your brother will not see it that way. And you probably will not be able to explain it to him that way either. At least not until everything settles down in a couple of days.

Imagine now a young married couple. They have two small children. The husband works overtime several nights a week. He says he's working overtime to make a little extra money to get ahead. He thinks that he's meeting his family responsibilities that way. The wife thinks he's shirking his family responsibilities by not being home with her and the children. What has happened in this case is that each person defines family responsibilities differently. This is another situation that can turn nasty unless both people are able to check reality with each other. They have to understand that each has a different interpretation of what fathers and mothers should do, and they have to work out a definition that they can agree on.

What has to happen in an intimate relationship is for the people involved to figure out what they expect from one another and to talk about it. Elizabeth Barrett Browning wrote: "How do I love thee? Let me count the ways." Well, there are probably as many ways of saying "I love you" as there are people who use the word. A comedian once commented that cannibals love their neighbors, too. So finding out what the other person thinks love means is important if you want to tell that person you love them. Some people, for example, think giving expensive presents shows love. Expensive presents just embarrass other people; they prefer small gifts, flowers, or letters. If two people with these different definitions get together, they will have to talk about what's going on or they will end up insulting one another instead of showing their affection.

When I'm sick I just like to be left alone. I don't want anyone fussing around and bothering me. My roommate thinks sick people shouldn't be left alone a minute. She keeps asking, "Do you want anything? Can I get you something to drink? Can I fluff the pillow? Would you like a book to read?" I hate it. I wish she would just go away and leave me alone. Worse, she expects me to take care of her like a baby if she even gets a cold. She gets real huffy if I don't pay enough attention to her. We're going to have to work something out or one of us is going to have to move.

Checking reality with the people you are close to is an important part of maintaining a transactional relationship. You do it by listening to find out what the other person thinks is important and is of value. If you want to tell people that you care about them, you have to find out what they think is a sign of caring about them. If you want to show them you're angry, you have to figure out what they will understand as anger. There is nothing worse than being truly furious and having someone make a remark like, "You're so cute when you yell like that." There are other ways of showing anger besides yelling. Maybe silence would get the point across.

In an interactional relationship you listen to find out what the rules and norms are so you could decide whether or not to conform. In a transactional relationship you listen to what the other person thinks, feels, and values. Then you can decide whether you can agree on how the relationship should be carried out. Some questions you will have to agree on are things such as how much time you will spend together, whether and how much space you will share, what activities you will undertake together, how you will reward one another, and how you will indicate displeasure to one another. You have to work out carefully a way to disagree without ending the relationship. It's like writing a contract or developing a constitution for your own little piece of the world.

Much of this kind of listening is paying attention to nonverbal cues that can tell you when the other person is comfortable or upset, angry or sad or satisfied. You listen for paralinguistic cues and you pay careful attention to silence. In a personal relationship what isn't said is often as important as what's said. Check back in the chapter on listening to understand for a refresher on how to listen to understand another person's feelings.

I suppose I should have known what was going on, but I didn't think about it. I knew that I didn't get many letters from my sister that year, and she was always so good at writing to me regularly. I only found out after she had filed for divorce that there was trouble. I wish now that I hadn't been so preoccupied. I should have noticed that she wasn't keeping in contact, and I might have called and gotten the story out of her before. Maybe I could have helped her somehow. I should have noticed the silence.

EMPATHIC LISTENING

Understanding other people is often called empathy. The dictionary defines empathy as "the intellectual identification of oneself with another." But we know that it's impossible to really know what someone else is thinking or feeling. It's impossible to get inside someone else's head or body. In *empathic listening* the best we can do is to try to imagine what someone else is thinking or feeling. There are two ways to go about this process: (1) We can recall similar experiences in our own lives and recall what we thought or felt in those situations, or (2) we can role-play the other person's situation by pretending to be him or her and imagining what that person must be thinking or feeling.

Dual Perspective

Let's consider a couple of examples to illustrate how you might use your imagination to gain a *dual perspective,* or an understanding of the situation from someone else's point of view. We will go back to the example of your imaginary brother who got home at 3:00 A.M. instead of midnight. Your parents were justifiably upset, but they might have reacted differently if they had looked at the situation from their son's point of view. All parents were young once (no matter how long ago). They might have spent some of the time they spent worrying remembering what had happened to them when they were young—how easy it is to forget the time when you're having fun. Instead of imagining horrible (and probably unlikely) scenarios, they might have remembered how defensive they felt when they realized that they were out later than they should have been. They probably reacted to their parents' scolding with anger; surely they will expect their own son to react the same way.

By using a process of dual perspective and remembering how they felt and acted when they were young, the parents might have chosen a different strategy when your brother came home late. Instead of yelling, they could have asked for an explanation first. Having listened carefully to that explanation, they could then have expected your brother to listen to their fears and anxieties on his behalf. The situation might have ended much differently if both parties had used dual perspective.

But, you will say, your brother can't remember what it was like to be old. He's never been old. How can he get a dual perspective, when he has no experience to call on? Your brother will have to use the second method of gaining dual perspective by imagining himself into the role of parent. It's not unlike acting. Pretend you are another person, and imagine what that person would feel like or act like. Pretend that you're sitting at home waiting for someone. Pretend he doesn't come after one hour, two hours, three hours. You don't know where he is. He might have had an accident. He might be injured. He might have forgotten you (that's an insulting thought, and you begin to get mad as well as worried). What would that person's feelings be? If your brother pretends for a few minutes to be a "parent," he might expect to get yelled at when he gets home so late. And he might listen quietly until he gets a turn to explain what really happened.

Have you ever stood in line at the post office for half an hour (or longer) to mail a package around Christmas time? Did you get frustrated and angry? And did you say something less than polite to the postal worker who seemed to you to be working as slowly as possible just to make your life difficult? Now stop and imagine you were that postal worker. You came to work in the morning knowing there was more work than you could get done in one day. Imagine standing for eight hours behind a counter, weighing packages and selling postage. By noon your legs and back ached, and you still have five hours to go. By 3:00 P.M. your head aches, too. You have to conserve your energy, because if you work too fast in the morning, by afternoon you will be too tired to work. You know that when you get tired, you make mistakes, and it's important not to make mistakes about people's Christmas packages. And you know people are going to be grumpy because they had to stand in line so long. If both parties in this situation took a dual perspective, they could make each other's lives much more pleasant.

Dual perspective is important both at work and in intimate relationships. It's a way of understanding one another better, so we can listen to find out what other people think and feel. If we use the process of dual perspective, by either remembering a similar experience or imagining ourselves in a strange situation, we can listen more effectively.

SYMPATHETIC LISTENING

Most of us look to our families and friends for emotional support in our lives. When we are ill they care for us, and when we are successful they help us celebrate. We spend important holidays with our families, sharing the rituals and emotions that make up family relationships. A lot of what we usually call emotional support is just having someone listen to us talk about our thoughts and feelings and working out our problems for ourselves. If our families don't share our feelings and values, we express our contempt by the statement, "Oh, they never listen to me anyway." That's almost the same thing as saying, "Oh, they don't care about me." There seems to be a close connection between caring and listening.

Think back to the last time you had to make a hard decision. Maybe it was the decision of whether or not to go to college. Or whether to move to another city. Or whether to get married or to leave a relationship. Whatever the decision was, you probably looked for someone who would just sit and listen to you talk out your problem. Sometimes that person is a family member, sometimes a friend, and sometimes that person is a professional listener like a psychologist or counselor. No matter who the person was who listened to your problems, you probably felt very close to that person and very grateful for his or her attention. Your relationship was strengthened by the experience.

If you want to create or maintain a relationship of emotional support with someone, you have to spend a good deal of time listening to that person talk about his or her life and experiences. Relationships are bargains in a sense; you listen to me and I listen to you. Part of that listening is gaining information about the other person, but a good part of the listening is just for its own sake. You may listen to the same stories, arguments, and problems over and over. You may have to listen to a lot of trivial details while the other person learns whether you can be trusted with important confidences. In any case the simple act of listening without judging is one of the most important bases of intimate relationships.

When you're listening to create or maintain a relationship with someone, you're focusing on the other person to find out about him or her. You aren't trying to get that individual to understand you, and you aren't trying to impress him or her or to score points. We all know there is nothing more boring than someone who's always talking about him or herself and who never listens and nothing is more flattering than being listened to. By listening to other people talk about their lives, you say to them, "I think you're an interesting and valuable person, and I want to know you better."

> I called up a guy from school to help me on a project. A friend of mine had said he knew some stuff about what I was writing about. Well, he spent over three hours telling me all about his life and what a great guy he was, and we never got around to the project at all. That guy is a slimy creep. If he had been a great guy he would have helped me with the project.

If someone asks you for emotional support, you have the right to decide whether or not to provide that support. Sometimes you can't. Maybe you don't really agree with this person or maybe the subject is too painful. Someone who has just lost a child or been through a divorce may not feel strong enough to listen to another person's pain. Sometimes you shouldn't. If your supervisor at work confides personal problems to you, he or she may be embarrassed about it later and you will be in trouble for knowing too much. You have no obligation to be a sympathetic listener unless you wish to. But if you do agree to provide emotional support, there are some general guidelines for sympathetic listening.

When you listen sympathetically you want the other person to feel that you understand him or her. One of the things you shouldn't do, therefore, is interrupt. Interrupting other people is a way of saying, "I'm not really interested in what you're saying; I want you to listen to me." That's a sure turnoff, especially for someone who's upset in any way. You can respond nonverbally, by nodding or smiling or saying things like "um hum" or "I see" to encourage the other person to keep talking. You do what seems appropriate at the time. Another thing you can do is to ask questions to make sure you really do understand what the other person is saying. These can be *mirror questions* that paraphrase what the other person said to check that you understood correctly. This is an example of a mirror question:

> "You are saying that you don't know how to tell your parents that you want to take a year off from college, because they have sacrificed so much to send you. But you feel like you're getting nowhere and you don't know what you really want to do in life. Is that what you're saying?"

You don't say whether you think your friend is right or wrong; you're just helping your friend clarify her feelings and thoughts. If you take a side—your friend should or shouldn't take a year off—the conversation may turn into an argument between the two of you. You will start arguing about what's right or wrong. That's not what you want; you want to help your friend make the best decision. You can do that by reflecting what you hear back to her and letting her make up her own mind. If you have a strong opinion, you can express that opinion at another time.

Sympathetic listening serves mostly to clarify the issues involved in problems or decisions. In the previous example the issues are that the friend feels frustrated in college but doesn't want to hurt her parents' feelings. She feels caught in a trap, torn between following her own wishes and complying with the wishes of her parents. She feels obligations to her parents, but also she feels obliged to act on her own. Once those issues are clarified, it will be easier for her to see what possible courses of action she has and how she might act. After the situation and the issues are clear, you can help your friend decide on a course of action by voicing your opinion. Before the situation is clear, it's your role to listen carefully and help your friend find her own feelings and ideas.

When you're listening sympathetically, you want to avoid doing things or saying things that will turn the other person off. Telling her what you would do in that situation shifts the focus from her to you and is a turnoff. Telling her that everyone feels that way sometimes is also a turnoff. It implies that her problems or feelings are trivial and not worth listening to. Asking the question "Why?" may put her on the spot and turn her off. And changing the subject is a clear cue to the other person that you don't want to listen anymore.

You may have noticed that *sympathetic listening* is really a kind of concentrated listening to understand. You are trying to understand another person's thoughts and feelings. So you can use the techniques of listening to understand. You can listen for the context of the situation. Is this problem something sudden, or has your friend been doubtful about college for some time? Is this concern something that regularly comes up about final exam time? Is something else in your friend's life causing her concern? Maybe a romance has gone wrong? Disagreements with her roommates? Often people who are upset get themselves into a kind of circular reasoning pattern where they go over and over the same feelings and ideas. By looking beyond that pattern of thinking, you can help your friend see her situation in a new light. By listening to identify your friend's feelings, you may help her understand herself better. And you should pay careful attention to what your friend is not saying. Are there some aspects of the situation that she's not talking about?

> I remember when I was going through the divorce, and I felt like each day was too much to bear. Every tiny decision was too difficult. I said to the counselor I was seeing, "I guess I'm doing all right. I'm coping." And she asked me, "What would it take to go beyond coping?" Well, that put a new light on things. I was able to think positively about the future instead of only being afraid that I would fail.

When you're trying to listen and reflect back to the speaker you should avoid statements using the words "I think" or "In my opinion" or "If I were you" or "It seems to me." Instead, you should begin statements with, "I hear you saying . . ." or "Do you mean . . ." or "I don't quite understand. Could you explain what you mean?" In this way you will avoid giving your opinion and focus on clarifying what the other person is thinking.

Your statements shouldn't contain words that evaluate: good, bad, smart, stupid, dumb, crazy, reasonable. Once you start agreeing or disagreeing or other-wise evaluating what the other person is saying, the focus is on you and not on him or her. You can't, for instance, contradict what the other person is saying even if you disagree. "Now you know that's not true" is the kind of evaluative statement that will either start an argument or cause the other person to shut up. You can ask questions like "Are you sure that's the way it is?" or "How do you know that's the way it is?" These statements can help the other person rethink his or her ideas without causing an argument. If someone is asking you for emotional support, telling that individual he or she is wrong is sure to be the wrong approach.

What you say should be tentative, not certain. You should offer your reflections, not force them on the speaker. So if you summarize what you have heard and the other person says, "No, no that's not what I'm saying at all," you don't respond with "Oh, yes, it is." That positive response would just start an argument and take attention away from the real focus of the conversation—clarifying the speaker's thoughts. If the speaker tells you that you have misunder-stood, you can say something like, "Well then, what were you saying?" And the focus of the conversation will stay where it belongs—on the situation under discussion and on the speaker's (and not your) thoughts.

Sympathetic listening is difficult to do, because it requires you not to speak and not to react with your own feelings and ideas. It requires that you listen and identify the feelings and ideas of the other person. Sympathetic listening is very valuable to you in building and maintaining relationships with your family and friends. If the difficulties of being a sympathetic listener are great, the rewards are also great. Some of the highest praise people give their friends is the statement: "I can talk to you about anything and you always understand." The result is often that your friend will then return the favor for you. And when you have an important problem to work out you will have someone who can help you sort it out by listening to you.

COMMUNICATION PRINCIPLES

Communication scholars have discovered and described several principles of communication that can help you in your personal and professional relationships with one another. In the last section of this chapter we discuss and illustrate several of these principles to show you how to use the knowledge.

You Can't Not Communicate

One of the important communication principles is that you can't *not* communi-cate. We understand that this sentence contains that dreaded grammatical error the double negative. But in this instance the double negative seems to express the thought best. What we mean when we say that "You can't not communicate" is that whenever you're in a relationship with another person, that person will be interpreting your behavior. Suppose, for example, that you have a friend who hasn't written or called you for a long time. You will interpret that fact—that the friend hasn't communicated by writing or calling—as indifference (I guess he doesn't want to be my friend anymore) or as distraction (I guess he must be real busy in his new job) or as something else (I wonder if he's having problems). The point is that you will attribute meaning to the lack of communication. If you wave to a friend who doesn't respond, you may conclude that you have been snubbed. The truth may be that the person didn't see you.

The observation that you can't not communicate holds true whenever you're in the presence of other people, even strangers. Take another common situation. You get on the elevator with someone you have never met before. If he speaks to you, you may conclude that he is friendly, and if he doesn't speak you may conclude that he is unfriendly. The point is you will draw some kind of conclusion about what kind of person he is whether he speaks or whether he doesn't speak. We are always interpreting other people's behavior as positive or negative toward us, even when they aren't even thinking about us. You can't not communicate.

Being aware of that communication principle, we can be more careful in our own interpretation of other people's behavior. We will understand that other people often act without having a conscious purpose to communicate with us. If you know that what you perceive may not be related to the other person's intention, you may think twice or recheck your perception before you act. Instead of getting mad because your friend didn't wave back, you may ask him, "Hey, didn't you see me downtown on Saturday? I waved to you and you just ignored me."

> My two roommates are "not speaking" again. They're mad about something. I hate it when they're "not speaking" because the silence sure is louder than any yelling they could do.

The Abstraction Principle

There is a commercial on the local television station that clearly illustrates another important communication principle that is associated with listening and personal relationships. The commercial is sponsored by a furniture store and features a young couple furnishing their first home. The husband says he can just see how the living room will look, and a picture appears showing a room furnished in early American maple furniture in shades of brown and green. The wife responds that she can see it too, but the picture changes to a contemporary look in chrome and glass in shades of blue and gold. The couple congratulate themselves on having come to an agreement so easily and move on to the bedroom. Here she pictures a French provincial room in white and pink, while the picture of the husband's idea shows something more austere in teak and dark plaid wool. But since neither partner actually described what he or she was thinking of, neither knows that the other is actually thinking of something quite different.

In our personal relationships we are often like the TV couple. We go on like they did believing that we are thinking alike until something happens to point out to us that we were only agreeing superficially. Since we didn't actually talk about the details of what we were thinking, we didn't know we were disagreeing. We stayed on an abstract level of thinking, instead of investigating the concrete bases for our statements.

When we generalize, we talk in *abstractions;* the concrete examples of what we are talking about are called *operational definitions.* Let's illustrate the difference between abstractions and operational definitions with some examples drawn from real life. The following statements were taken from an employees' handbook for employees of a grocery store chain. In that handbook there was one page of pledges of what the company would do for the employee, and another page of store regulations to govern the behavior of employees at work. See if you can pick out which statements are generalizations and which are operational definitions.

The Company Pledge

To express the conviction and promise that this company will be a good place to work, we pledge:

1. That every individual employee will be treated fairly with consideration and respect, both as persons and participants in the success of the company's future.
2. That everyone who supervises the work of others, at whatever level, is continually expected to treat those under their direction as they themselves would want to be treated.
3. To pay wages and provide benefits that equitably reward employees for their skill, effort, time, seniority, and dedication.
4. To weigh all decisions with regard to their effect on the well-being of the employees.

Store Regulations

1. You are not permitted to ring up a sale for merchandise you purchase.
2. Insubordination or refusal to follow specific instruction of a supervisor is cause for dismissal.
3. No eating or chewing of gum on the floor.
4. Employees must leave the store at all times through the front entrance. Employees are advised that they may be asked to open their parcels, shopping bags, or purses for security checks.

It's pretty clear that the company pledge is a series of abstractions that really hold the company to nothing. They sound good, but they don't really say anything. The store regulations, on the other hand, are operational definitions; there is no question about what employees may and may not do.

Some examples of incidents in the store can help explain the differences. One day an employee of the store, the manager of the cosmetics section, was taking inventory after the store was closed. She was sitting on the floor counting the small items on the bottom shelves. Her supervisor came by and reminded her that employees were not allowed to sit on the floor. She replied that she was tired and the store was closed and she intended to sit on the floor. She was fired. What about the company pledge that employees would be treated fairly with consideration and respect, you say? Never mind, store regulations state that refusal to follow a specific instruction is grounds for dismissal.

Let's look at another example related to the company pledge that the company would pay wages and provide benefits equitably. In fact, the store never hired anyone full time; every employee worked 38 or 39 hours. In that way the store avoided having to pay health and unemployment benefits to employees, saving the company a good deal of money. Was that fair and equitable to the employees? It depends on what you mean by "fair and equitable." Those words are abstractions, and unless they are spelled out in specific operational definitions, they can be interpreted any way you wish.

For every generalization, there are any number of different ways to define operationally what you mean. That's why abstractions are dangerous: You may be thinking of one operational definition while I am thinking of one that's completely different. The following are some common generalizations that people use all the time. In the first example, we have provided several possible operational definitions. See if you can find operations definitions for the other abstract statements:

Abstraction	Operational Definition
1. You have a bad attitude.	1. You never smile at me.
	2. You work too slowly.
	3. You don't say positive things.
	4. You don't talk much.
2. He is nervous.	1._____
	2._____
	3._____
3. I feel lousy.	1._____
	2._____
	3._____
4. She's a jerk.	1._____
	2._____
	3._____

Hopefully, from these examples you can see the many ways in which talking in abstractions or generalizations can get you in trouble in your relationships, both at home and at work. It's important to reach an understanding on what you mean, and to do that, you need to find and agree on operational definitions. One of the important functions of labor unions is to insist on operational definitions of pay and working conditions for their members. In personal relationships like the young couple buying furniture, individuals have to negotiate an agreement on important issues between themselves. Being aware of abstractions can help you become a better listener and help you improve your relationships.

You Really Gotta Wanna

This isn't a formal communication principle, but we think it should become one. The statement means that knowing *how* to be an effective listener is no guarantee that you will behave effectively. It depends on whether you make the effort, whether you "wanna." Many people who can play musical instruments never do so; they don't wanna. It takes a lot of time and dedication to keep in practice and to perform, whether it's playing music or being a good listener.

Diana Garland (1981) reported a study she did on counseling married couples by teaching them listening skills that illustrates this principle very well. She studied a group of married couples who were attending counseling sessions to improve their marriages. Half of them received instruction in listening skills to help them understand their partner better. The other half received no listening training. What Garland learned was that the couples who received the training could, in fact, identify what the other person was thinking and feeling more often than the couples who didn't get the training. *But they weren't any more successful in counseling than the people who received no training.* Garland concluded that the couples who were trained knew how to understand one another better, but they just chose not to. They didn't want to.

The point should be quite clear. Listening to maintain relationships is hard work. It takes time and thought, and it's often frustrating. Unless you are committed to the relationship, you may not make the effort. You really have to want to. We could outline the best program of listening training, and we could have you practice until you were perfect. But if you didn't choose to put those skills to work in your own life, you would leave the training in the classroom and go out into the world as inept as you were before you were trained. That's one of the problems of compelling employees to take communication training. Unless they want to make the effort, they will not improve. The same thing goes for personal relationships, as we illustrated in the preceding case study.

The fact is that you can't listen to maintain a relationship once and have it done with. It's like dusting the house; you have to do it over and over again every day, every week, every month, and every year. Because people grow, develop, and change, their lives change and we have to keep up with those changes to maintain relationships. Businesses that can't keep up with the changes in their environment go bankrupt, and couples who don't keep up with the changes in one another's lives drift apart. Relationships need constant attention; you have to have commitment to the other person and to the relationship to keep listening.

SUMMARY

In this chapter we illustrated how listening skills related to personal relationships at home and at work. We talked about two different kinds of relationships: interactions, or public relationships governed by formal rules, and transactions, or private relationships negotiated between individuals. We showed the importance of listening to check reality of both types of relationships. We explained how taking a dual perspective—by looking at the situation from the other person's point of view—can help you be a better listener. We explained the role of sympathetic listening in personal relationships and gave some pointers on how to listen sympathetically. We illustrated important communication principles that can help you listen better to maintain relationships: the abstraction principle, you can't not communicate, and you really gotta wanna.

SUGGESTED ACTIVITIES

1. Keep a listening log of your speaking and listening behavior with your family and best friends for a week. Write down approximately what amount of time you spend talking and what amount of time you spend listening to each person. Analyze the log and see if any patterns emerge. Are there people you always listen to or do other people spend their time listening to you?

2. Interview a person who's a trained listener, a counselor or psychologist, for example. Ask about the training in listening and about the techniques that he or she finds useful in his or her work.

3. Analyze the norms for a group of which you're a member. Try to figure out what the unwritten rules for behavior in that group are. Are there rules about who's to speak and who's to listen? Are there rules about which topics are appropriate and which aren't appropriate for discussion in the group? What are the consequences of not following the norms in the group?

4. Go to the local shopping area or mall and wander through the stores where clerks aren't always behind the counters. How can you recognize the clerks? Do they have distinctive ways of dressing? distinctive ways of walking? Do they have distinctive patterns of what they say?

REFERENCES AND RECOMMENDED READING

Bate, Barbara. *Communication and the Sexes.* New York: Harper & Row, 1986.

Caplow, Theodore. *Managing an Organization.* New York: Holt, Rinehart and Winston, 1983.

Eakins, Barbara Westbrook, and R. Gene Eakins. *Sex Differences in Human Communication.* Boston: Houghton Mifflin, 1978.

Galvin, Kathleen, and Bernard J. Brommel. *Family Communication.* Glenview, IL: Scott, Foresman, 1982.

Garland, Diana R. "Training Married Couples in Listening Skills: Effects on Behavior, Perceptual Accuracy and Marital Adjustment." *Family Relations* 30 (1981): 297–306.

Gilligan, Carol. *In a Different Voice.* Cambridge, MA: Harvard University Press, 1982.

Goodall, H. Lloyd, Jr., and Gerald M. Phillips. *Making It in Any Organization.* Englewood Cliffs, NJ: Prentice-Hall, 1984.

Knapp, Mark L. *Nonverbal Communication in Human Interaction.* New York: Holt, Rinehart and Winston, 1972.

Peck, M. Scott. *The Road Less Traveled.* New York: Simon & Schuster, 1978.

Phillips, Gerald M., and H. Lloyd Goodall, Jr. *Living and Loving.* Englewood Cliffs, NJ: Prentice-Hall, 1983.

Verderber, Rudolph F., and Kathleen S. *Interact* (3rd Edition). Belmont, CA: Wadsworth, 1984.

chapter 6

Listening to Decide

When you have finished reading this chapter you should be able to:

1. Define critical listening and describe its importance in decision making.
2. Distinguish between emotional and rational arguments.
3. Describe how emotional persuasion works.
4. Name and describe six common emotional appeals.
5. Name and describe three parts of a rational argument.
6. Identify and explain three kinds of evidence.
7. Identify and explain three criteria to evaluate expert opinion.
8. Name and describe four common reasoning patterns.
9. Describe propaganda and distinguish it from rational persuasion.
10. Name and describe six common propaganda appeals.

When you have finished reading this chapter you should be able to define these concepts:

1. emotional persuasion
2. rational persuasion
3. validity
4. argument
5. claim, reasoning pattern, evidence
6. fact, inference, judgment
7. cause/effect, induction, deduction, analogy

8. propaganda
9. bandwagon, testimonial, mudslinging, card-stacking

Making decisions is something we have to do every day. From deciding when to get up, what to wear, and whether to eat breakfast, we go on to more consequential decisions about what career to prepare for, whether or when to get married, or how to finance a new home. We decide issues that are important to the community and the nation by voting in elections for particular proposals or persons.

In a free society decision making is the privilege and responsibility of every individual. Although we know this because we have heard it said all our lives, most of us haven't considered the alternative. In many societies decisions are made for people by custom or tradition, or by the machinery of the state. In India, for instance, most people are born into a caste which determines their social position and the occupations that are open or closed to them. In China people do not decide where they will live; the government assigns them to communities. By another government policy Chinese couples do not decide how many children to have; they are limited to one child. In South Africa race determines the place of residence, occupation, and political rights. We know that in our own country, decisions are often constrained by forces beyond our control. There is racial and ethnic prejudice, and many choices are constrained by economic opportunities. But in the United States, choices aren't officially proscribed and prejudice isn't officially sanctioned. We really are to a large extent responsible for running our own lives. We have to make decisions.

The study of decision making in a free society has an extensive history, stretching from the ancient Greek study of rhetoric to modern behaviorism and artificial intelligence. But instead of reviewing such studies, we will concentrate on the kinds of decisions you as an individual may make in your daily life, and how your listening behaviors may affect the decisions you make.

You make many kinds of decisions: personal, social, business, professional, political. In making these decisions you're often influenced by both emotional and rational considerations. In this section we explain how emotional appeals provide a poor basis for making important decisions. Emotional appeals bypass the thinking process, and you can be fooled into false conclusions by attending to these appeals. Rational appeals, on the other hand, are carefully constructed arguments based on logic and on evidence. By listening critically to the basis for rational arguments, you can evaluate their validity or truth. In this chapter we show you how to discriminate between emotional and rational appeals. We teach you to identify logical arguments and to evaluate the evidence used to support those arguments. We teach you to listen critically.

EMOTIONAL PERSUASION

Emotional persuasion is based on appeal to our feelings. It's a very powerful persuasion, because it's very difficult to argue against our feelings. Most emotional persuasion, in fact, takes the form of nonverbal appeal; images and music play a large part in creating feelings that can persuade us.

Music in Persuasion

In ancient times people used music in magical dances designed to persuade the gods to favor their requests. They had rain dances, fertility dances, and war dances. Military music, in the form of marching music, has been used for centuries to stir up people's feelings and incite them to action. Armies used to march into battle accompanied by the drum and fife or the bagpipes. What would a parade be today without the music of a big brass band?

Music is used to create many different moods. Lullabies have lulled babies to sleep for centuries. In a more practical application of that idea, moviemakers and television producers commonly use "mood music" to accompany the action and help create appropriate feelings in audiences. Contemporary television shows like *Miami Vice* have brought the use of mood music almost to a high art, with the music incorporated into the plot itself. Dentists' offices and elevators feature soothing music, while shopping centers and supermarkets play happy music to induce you to buy more. To turn the concept around, we have created rock videos, with images created to accompany the music.

> I remember watching a talk show on television, and the featured guest was a composer who wrote music for the movies. To illustrate what music can do, he showed a clip of a movie with Burt Reynolds in a chase scene. "Good old" Burt was in a speedboat being chased by a helicopter. The composer showed the clip three times with different kinds of music and that same scene was suspenseful (you didn't know if Burt would get away), exhilarating (you were sure Burt would make it), and hilariously funny (it was all a gag). Mood music really does make a difference.

In more recent times rock and roll has been a controversial kind of music, because some people have claimed that rock rhythms can incite violent and sexual feelings in young people. Whether or not those claims are true, it's true that music appeals directly to our emotions and can be used as a powerful persuader.

Images in Persuasion

Images function in much the same way as music to appeal directly to our feelings without the mediation of words. Artists have studied the effects of color, shape, and line on our feelings and learned to create images that will affect us in predictable ways. Vertical and horizontal lines, for example, give a feeling of stability, whereas diagonal lines are dynamic and give us a feeling of movement and change. Bright primary colors excite our feelings, whereas the paler colors or neutral colors induce a quieter mood. Interior decorators utilize these principles in decorating public buildings and private homes.

Advertisers and public relations experts haven't been slow to pick up on the power of images to affect our emotions. Advertisers use images to portray their products in a favorable light, so we will want to buy their products. Did you ever notice that the cigarette advertisements, which are required by law to include a warning that smoking is hazardous to your health, often feature pictures of healthy, happy young people engaging in active sports? The image in the advertisement directly contradicts, and possibly overpowers, the warning message placed inconspicuously in the corner of the picture. Actions, as they say, often speak louder than words.

Pictures of beautiful children are regularly used to induce us to give money to support medical research for birth defects or childhood diseases. Pictures of starving children induce us to donate money to charities. Images of big-eyed baby seals persuade us to oppose seal hunting and to buy cloth coats instead of fur coats. The images on television of the violence in the Vietnam War are widely credited with having persuaded the American people to support the antiwar sentiment. Images and music are powerful persuaders.

Verbal Emotional Appeals

But images and music aren't the only emotional appeals; we can also find emotional appeals in the spoken or written word. By speaking in such a way as to induce us to have certain feelings, while discouraging us from thinking carefully about what we heard, artful speakers can persuade us to believe what they say. You will get a better idea of how this works by considering a few examples. Some of the most common emotional appeals used by speakers and writers include appeals to patriotism, appeals to pride, appeals to fear, appeals to elitism, appeals to fads, and guilt. We will illustrate how each of these works.

Appealing to emotions is both subtle and effective. When we listen with our emotions, we stop thinking and judging. We can be led to act against our own best judgment and even against our own best interest by unscrupulous emotional persuaders. Jim Jones led his followers to commit suicide and to kill their own children through the use of powerful emotional appeals. Emotional appeals are very dangerous. While ethical speakers may occasionally use emotional appeals, you must be very suspicious of anyone who relies entirely on emotional appeals to persuade you.

Patriotism　　Appeals to patriotism are common. Most recently we heard appeals to patriotism to induce us to send money for the renovation of the Statue of Liberty. Although there is nothing wrong with feeling proud of our country, we need to be wary of letting our feelings take the place of our reason. "America First" kinds of appeals imply that as Americans we can't be wrong, so anything we do must be right. In the late 1960s we often saw bumper stickers that said "America—Love It or Leave It." This slogan was a response to the anti-Vietnam War movement. The implication was that if you didn't blindly follow whatever the government decided—in this case to send American soldiers to fight in Vietnam—you were unpatriotic. That kind of thinking implies that there is only one kind of "Americanism" and only one way of being a good American. Surely this wasn't the idea the Founding Fathers had when they set up our representative government. Dissent is the right of patriots in a free society.

> Until you have lived in a different society, I don't think you can appreciate the freedom we have in the United States. We lived in Tehran for two years in the early 1970s, and I remember trying to have a conversation about building a subway system in Tehran. There was some controversy about the project, because the city is built on sand, and there's no sewer system. But my Iranian Army friends couldn't talk about it. They said, "His Imperial Majesty has decided Tehran is to have a subway. If we speak against it, someone may hear us and turn us in. We could be punished." I was shocked, I can tell you. Imagine not being able even to discuss something our president had decided. We are so lucky.

We also often hear "Buy American" appeals urging us to buy only American products. We usually hear these kinds of appeals when foreign-made products of equal or better quality can be bought cheaper. Since the advertisers can't claim to have a better or a cheaper product, they are reduced to using appeals to patriotism to get people to buy their products. Claims that buying American products keeps Americans employed are also irrelevant to the actual value of the product. Changing the subject is a sneaky way of avoiding the issue, not a rational way of arguing.

When you hear appeals to patriotism, you should be wary of letting your feelings rule your better judgment. Consider if there are logical reasons for deciding to believe something or to act. Remember that America was built on the idea that we come to truth by listening to many different kinds of opinions. There are many different ways of being a good American, so the claim that Americanism can be identified with one idea or one product is invalid.

Pride It's a good thing to be proud of our families, our heritage, our communities, our own achievements. We all like to feel that we are important and valuable and good. But appeals to pride are sometimes used to stop us from thinking and to believe as the speaker or writer wishes us to believe. Aren't you proud of your family? Don't they deserve the best? Then you should . . . buy this kind of toilet tissue . . . feed them Rifton's New and Improved Cereal . . . buy lots of life insurance . . . or whatever. It doesn't matter whether you actually need more life insurance or whether the cereal is tasty and nutritious. And what does pride have to do with toilet tissue? Nothing. It's simply an appeal that will (hopefully) flatter you into buying the product.

Appeals to pride are often used by politicians seeking votes. Politicians claim special ties to ethnic groups—appealing to their pride in their heritage—to get people to vote for them. They tout their Irish ancestry, or claim to love Polish sausage, or tell us some of their best friends are Jewish or black. They used to get themselves made honorary Indian chiefs, until the Indians got wise to them. We should get wise to them, too.

Of course, we all want the best for our families and our communities. But we need to decide what's best by thinking and considering alternatives logically, not by responding to emotional appeals. You don't always have to buy the top of the line, and you don't have to keep up with the next-door neighbors. We should be careful of flattery, especially from people who want us to believe or do something that will clearly benefit them.

Fear   Fear is a tricky appeal to make, but when it's done well it can be very effective. Thousands of people in the late 1950s built bomb shelters in their backyards against the threat of nuclear war. We now know that backyard shelters are ineffective. But the fear was real at the time, and made a lot of money for some people. The same kind of irrational fear—that of Communists and communism—led to the McCarthyism of the 1950s, an event in American history that should sober us all. Many people's reputations were ruined and hundreds of people lost their jobs when they were falsely accused of being Communists. Fear is a powerful appeal, and we must be very careful to avoid acting on irrational fears.

Some fears are normal and rational, and action taken to avoid disaster may be justified. So we buy auto insurance and home insurance to protect us against the loss of our most important financial assets. But we can't protect ourselves against every possible contingency, and we have to weigh the chances of disaster against the cost of protection. That's what the debate about the cost of the Defense Department budget is about. How much money must we spend to keep our nation safe from enemy attack? How many fighter jets and bombers, aircraft carriers and nuclear submarines do we need? How many missiles? As many as the Russians have? Twice as many? How many do they have anyway? How do we know that? It's very easy to get carried away by our fears and to spend more than we can afford, while shorting our nation in other ways.

Often it's harder to see the very real dangers to the nation in lack of health care for the poor or lack of support for education programs than to see the less likely but more lurid dangers of involvement in global thermonuclear war. We have to weigh carefully the evidence when we make decisions about how to spend our money. Although it's often hard to wait for all the evidence to be in, we need to practice patience and make sure of the facts before we act out of fear.

Last Christmas they hired two or three extra clerks at the card store where I was working. One of the young women worked full time for an insurance company; she was working part time during Christmas to pick up extra money. I asked her what kind of insurance her company sold, expecting her to say automobile insurance or home insurance. Her answer shocked me. She said, "We rip off old people." Her company sold life insurance and health insurance to senior citizens. The old people were especially susceptible to appeals about health care costs; they knew they could easily be bankrupt by a single serious illness. Or they were concerned for the welfare of the wife or husband who would be left alone after their death. The company this woman worked for knew that and used those fears to make money, selling them expensive policies they didn't need. I was glad I didn't work for a company like that!

Elitism   Elitism is an appeal that's closely related to pride, but it appeals more to what people would like to be than to their real history or heritage. We envy the rich and famous people we read about in the popular magazines or see in movies and on television. So we buy products they say they use, so we can be like them. We do exercises to look like Jane Fonda, or work out at the gym to look like Mr. Universe. Clothing with designer labels sells for three or four times what it's actually worth. And any chemist will tell you that there are only a limited number of chemicals that go into any cosmetic product. Most of the chemicals are simple and cheap. When you buy famous (and expensive) cosmetics, what you're buying is the brand name, and the appeal to elitism—making someone else rich by trying to be better than other people.

Another place where the appeal to elitism is very sinister is in college sports. College athletes are often treated almost like royalty. They have special dining halls, special medical attention, special academic coaching. They receive special scholarships, and they have a very high status on campus. You might even get the idea that they are better people than the nonathletes in your classes. And you would be wrong. College isn't about athletics; it's about scholarship. Many of the college athletes who think they are going to make it big in professional sports find they can't make the grade. Even if they don't get injured, there simply aren't enough slots on the professional teams for all the college athletes. But in the meantime they have managed to get through classes without learning, and they don't have an education either. They are victims of appeals to elitism.

Elitism also shows its ugly head in college social life. Some sororities and fraternities are considered "better" than others, and to belong to the "best" organizations becomes almost an obsession with some students. Some people feel their college careers (college careers?) will be ruined if they don't get into the organization of their choice. Fewer students, but still a sizable number, make their grade point average the most important goal of their lives. These people spend all their time pursuing the elusive 4.0; they forget that learning is the goal of education and not some abstract number that has no meaning once they get out of college. What happens to these people when they leave college? They discover that no one in the working world cares much about their grade point average in college. And membership in the most elite social fraternity will not get them a raise or a promotion; only knowledge and effort will.

When we make decisions about how to live our lives, we have to be careful about what we decide is important. A good yardstick to use when making this judgment is to look at a ten-year period of time. Is what you want today going to be equally as important to you in ten years? Or, is there something else you should be thinking about? Keeping a sense of perspective will help you avoid being taken in by appeals to elitism.

Faddism   Fads have always been around. For a while everyone is eating pasta with pesto, and then it's goat cheese and sundried tomatoes and anchovy. Lite beer and wine coolers are in, since people have stopped drinking hard liquor so much. Blue jeans, traditionally work clothing for people who worked outdoors, suddenly became fashionable at any social occasion. And wearing hats went out for a while, but now it seems to be back in. Television advertising is the source of much of the faddism, and Saturday morning is the time to look for the examples of this type of ad. Watch the toy ads and see how cleverly the advertisers imply that *you* should have this wonderful toy because *everyone else* in you neighborhood will have one. That's the basic appeal of faddism.

There is nothing really wrong with fads; sometimes it's fun to do something new and interesting. And, in fact, some things that started out as fads have proved to be useful and healthful innovations. Runners and joggers have ceased to be a novelty, and all of us are now aware of the necessity of a regular exercise program to keep us healthy. We could say the same about diet. Most of us eat more fiber and less fat, more fruits and vegetables and less sugar, and we are careful about salt. That's all to the good, and we will be healthier for being careful of our diets.

But fads, like everything, can be taken to an extreme. There are all kinds of crazy diets on the market that appeal to people who want to lose weight without effort or pain. Some of those diets are merely foolish, and some are downright dangerous. Exercise is good for you, but running and handball aren't for everyone. Taking up a new diet or exercise plan isn't something you should do just because everyone else is doing it.

> I was in the department store the other day and I overheard a conversation between a mother and a nine-year-old boy. He was trying on these lurid short pants—green and red and orange and blue geometric designs—and she was saying wearily, "But, Brian, don't you think you have enough jamms? I've already spent $95.00 on your pants this week." I couldn't believe it. A hundred dollars for weird pants? On my budget, that hundred dollars was three weeks worth of food. Boy, somebody's making a lot of money off that fad!

A few years ago millions of people spent thousands of dollars on CBs. Now as many have personal computers they never really learned to use. Hundreds of people have gone to foreign countries and spent their life savings on questionable cures for cancer. Before you undertake a new program of diet or exercise, before you invest your money in a surefire get-rich-quick scheme, before you buy a product that you don't really need, you should stop and think about what you're doing. When you stop and think, you quit listening to your emotions. And you may save yourself a lot of money or even save your life.

Guilt   Guilt is another sneaky appeal that people can make on your emotions. This appeal is often used to separate us from our money for "worthy" causes. It's a complex issue, because we don't want to suggest that there aren't really worthy causes that could make good use of money we could afford to give. We are saying that truly worthy causes—Boy Scouts and Girl Scouts, Salvation Army, Red Cross, the public radio or television station, the local ambulance service, the community library—all base their appeals for our charity on their own record of service. These are rational appeals, supported by evidence of the benefit derived from our donations. These groups can say to you, "See what benefits we provide for the community; please support our cause." These groups can also show you how their money is spent.

Charities and worthy causes that can't show concrete results are forced into making emotional appeals geared toward making you feel guilty about being more fortunate than other people. Pictures of starving children move us to pity, and sometimes move us to get out our wallets and give money. In doing so, we may feel better, but we wouldn't feel so good if we found out the money went into someone else's pocket instead of to the children. Unfortunately that's exactly what too often happens.

> A few years ago, when there were so many appeals for help for the starving Ethiopians, we were all caught up in the spirit of the thing. Millions of people gave money to Live Aid. Nobody questioned how that money would be spent; they just wrote out their checks. I remember reading about a man in Los Angeles who raised over $200,000 for Ethiopian aid and then disappeared to Mexico with the money. It makes you sick.

When you hear appeals for your money or your time that make you feel sorry for others, stop and think whether this is a situation for which you're in any way responsible. Then think whether your time or money would make a difference. Unfortunately money can't cure every problem. Don't decide on the basis of your feelings whether or not the appeal is worthy. Ask for facts. Ask for evidence. Then decide whether or not you want to help. Helping others who need our help is a good thing; but helping others to get rich at our expense is foolish behavior.

The very power of emotional persuasions constitutes a great danger, because they can be used by unscrupulous manipulators to deceive us into false beliefs. Because we are persuaded without reasoning, by direct appeals to our feelings, we seldom think to judge the legitimacy of the causes for or against which we are being persuaded. When we see pictures of starving children, we are unlikely to ask ourselves whether our contributions will go directly to the children or whether they will end up in the pockets of some crook running a false charity. We are unlikely to ask about the causes of the conditions that led to starvation and whether our contributions will have any direct effect on those causes. We skip the reasoning steps between cause and effect that would lead us to think logically about the situation.

What, you will say, does all this have to do with listening? This is, after all, a listening book, isn't it? The answer is that our best and possibly only defense against being manipulated by emotional appeals is to listen critically to the claims being made by the persuaders. When we listen critically we don't just react, we stop and think. We stop and think about the meaning of what we see or hear and we judge the validity of the claims. We figure out the logical patterns in what's being said and we evaluate the evidence to support what's being claimed. When we listen critically we look for rational arguments and we require evidence to support those arguments. We aren't influenced blindly by others; we make up our own minds.

RATIONAL PERSUASION

Rational persuasion is a thinking process; it doesn't appeal to your feelings or emotions. Rational persuasion uses words; you can't do it in pictures or music. *Rational persuasion* is a verbal process of stating a claim and making an argument to support that claim. Rational appeals are made by talking or writing; understanding rational appeals is done by listening and thinking. In this section we illustrate how to listen to arguments and how to think about them and decide whether or not to believe them.

As people usually use the word, *argument* means disagreement. But we are using argument in a technical sense to mean a claim supported by reasoning and evidence. Rational argument involves three things: (1) a claim, (2) a reasoning pattern, and (3) evidence. First we define and explain these terms, and then we illustrate the process of critical listening by using an example.

First of all, a *claim* is simply a statement that someone wants you to believe. "Nifty Hairspray is the best" would be an example of a claim. *Evidence* refers to the facts used to support or prove the claim. *Validity* refers to truth or soundness of a claim. We might find that 50 people had tried Nifty Hairspray and 45 people had liked it. That example would stand as evidence for the claim that Nifty Hairspray was the best. To connect the evidence with the claim, we use a reasoning pattern or a logical connection. In this case the reasoning pattern between the claim—Nifty Hairspray is the best—and evidence used to support that claim—50 people tried it and 45 of them said they liked it—is an inductive pattern. We explain more about reasoning patterns later in this chapter.

Evidence: Facts, Inferences, and Judgments

We need to understand that evidence comes in different kinds. There are facts, inferences, and judgments. The best evidence is, of course, facts, but facts are very hard to come by. *Facts* are verifiable; you can validate, identify, and measure facts. "The temperature is 95 degrees and the humidity is 80 percent," is a statement of fact, because we can measure both temperature and humidity. "I think it will rain today," would be an inference, because we don't know if it will rain. An *inference* is a prediction based on experience. Because it has usually rained when it was very hot and the humidity was very high (and there were angry black clouds in the sky), we infer that it will probably rain this time. We have to make inferences about what has happened when we weren't there and what may happen in the future, because these things are impossible to verify. Finally, "It's too hot to work," is a judgment. A *judgment* is a statement of preference, and we would prefer not to have to work when it's so hot and humid. As a rule, judgments don't make good evidence, except when they are made by experts about a subject that the experts are knowledgeable about.

The problem with facts, inferences, and judgments is that although they are different logical categories—in that they are different kinds of statements—the statements actually look very similar. Sometimes we are deceived by the form of the sentence into thinking that judgments are facts and are valid claims. The statement "William has a bad attitude" sounds very much like the statement "William has brown eyes." But the statement about brown eyes is a fact, because we can verify that statement by comparing William's eyes to color samples and discovering that they are brown. But the statement about William's attitude is a judgment; it simply means the speaker doesn't like something William is doing. An attitude can't be identified and measured. When you listen critically, you must be able to identify whether the speaker is using facts, inferences, or judgments as evidence.

Now that you know something about evidence, let's take an example and test your critical listening skills. Let's consider the hypothetical case of a community in which a special interest group has proposed a new ordinance banning the sale of pornography in all city bookstores. The ordinance must be voted on by the city council, and there will be an open meeting to discuss the proposal. As a concerned citizen you will have to make up your mind whether or not you support the proposal. The proposition is as follows:

> We should ban the sale of pornography in all city bookstores, because pornography is evil and it causes violence and sexual abuse.

Expert Opinion As Evidence   In support of the claim that pornography should be banned, we are presented with two bits of evidence. The first is the statement that pornography is evil. Is this statement a fact, an inference, or a judgment? If you said it's a judgment, you were right. The statement represents the opinion of some people; we can't identify and measure evil. When we are presented with judgments as evidence, we have to decide whether or not the judgment is valid. We have to know whether or not to believe it. So how do we decide whether or not to accept this judgment as valid?

We can ask ourselves questions about opinions or judgments that can lead us to decide whether or not we agree with them. There are three questions to ask:

1. Who says? Identify the individuals making the statements.
2. What's their experience with the subject?
3. What's their character and reputation?

In this case the answer to the first question is that various clergy and citizens say pornography is evil. The answer to the second question is not clear. We don't know what their experience with the subject is. And the answer to the last question is that some of the people have a high standing in the community and a reputation for honesty and integrity. In order to accept opinion as evidence to support a claim, you should be able to answer all three questions; you only want to accept the opinion of qualified experts as evidence. We don't know whether the people who say pornography is evil are qualified experts, because we don't know what their experience with the subject is. We should look for further evidence on which to judge the merits of this proposal. So we can't accept the statement that pornography is evil as evidence to support the proposal.

Research Results As Evidence   Since we couldn't accept the claim that pornography is evil, let's look at the second bit of evidence: Pornography causes violence and sexual abuse. We don't understand the connection, so we ask the people who proposed the resolution how they came to that conclusion. They cite a study done by researchers who found that all the prison inmates they questioned admitted to reading pornography. From this research study the researchers concluded that reading pornography caused the criminals to commit violent acts and sexual abuse. We must discover what kind of argument this is and whether the argument is valid.

The researchers have used a very common type of argument—the cause/ effect argument. All the criminals they questioned admitted to reading pornography; therefore, pornography was at least a partial cause of their criminal behavior. But is this a correct use of the reasoning? If we think carefully, we will discover that there are probably also many people who read pornography but who aren't criminals and who aren't in prison for committing violent acts. And if we examine the study, we will discover that the prisoners who were studied were all men. What about women who commit violent acts? Did they also read pornography? If we reason carefully, we will find that there is no valid basis for the cause/effect argument that reading pornography causes people to commit violent and abusive acts. It may, but we don't have enough evidence to prove that it does.

After listening critically to the arguments for the proposal to eliminate pornography from the bookstores and newsstands, we have discovered that the rational arguments do not stand up. We can find no evidence to support the claims made by the supporters of the proposal. This doesn't necessarily mean that the proposal isn't a good one. It only means that if we want to decide whether or not to support the proposal, we will have to look elsewhere for evidence on which to decide.

Common Reasoning Patterns

The reasoning behind this proposal was cause/effect reasoning, but that's not the only possible reasoning pattern that could be used. There are four common reasoning patterns that you should be able to recognize. These reasoning patterns are (1) cause/effect, (2) induction, (3) deduction, and (4) analogy. We define each of these patterns and provide some examples to make them clearer.

Cause/Effect Reasoning   *Cause/effect* reasoning simply says that when one thing happens, something else always follows. Your parents and teachers tell you that if you study hard, you will get good grades. Studying causes good grades. But if you have bad study habits, no amount of studying is going to get you better grades. Cause/effect arguments about human behavior are usually not so strong as cause/effect arguments applied in other contexts. A much stronger case could be made that bacteria cause infections. Whenever someone gets an infection, laboratory tests can find bacteria in the tissue samples. And if we put bacteria into healthy tissue samples, those samples soon develop infections. So we conclude that bacteria cause infections.

Induction   *Induction* is a reasoning pattern going from specific examples to a general principle. A teacher might notice that those students who sit in the front row always seem to get better grades than students who sit in the back row. From her own experience, she will conclude that sitting in the front row is related in some way to good grades. Without saying why students in the front row get good grades (maybe they can hear better, or maybe they don't goof around so much?), she will know the two things are connected. This is an example of an inductive pattern of reasoning. But if we find some cases where students who sit in the front row do not get better grades, we would want to examine her hypothesis.

   Most of our knowledge of medical practice is based on inductive principles. Physicians noticed that people had similar symptoms and similar outcomes in their illnesses. They named those illnesses and began looking for causes and cures. Doctors now know that people have suffered and died of what is called Legionnaires Disease for years before the pattern was noticed in a number of cases in a convention hotel. Now we have a new disease with a recognized diagnosis and treatment. That's the way much scientific knowledge is built.

Deduction   Deduction is the opposite of induction; *deduction* takes a general principle and applies it to a specific instance. The same teacher who noticed that students in the front row got good grades tells another teacher about this observation. The second teacher believes the claim. When one of his students asks how to improve her grades, the second teacher suggests that she sit in the front row. He has taken the generalization "Students who sit in the front row get good grades" and applied it to the instance of the student who asked how to improve her grades. He used deductive reasoning.

   When physicians prescribe a course of treatment, they are using deductive logic. They have examined the patient and decided on a diagnosis by a deductive process. If this case resembles the cases described in the medical books, the physician deduces that this patient has that disease. And then she uses another deductive process to prescribe treatment. If antibiotics have worked for other people with this disease, she prescribes the same antibiotics for this patient— deducing that what worked for others will work for this patient.

Analogy   Finally, there is a fourth common reasoning pattern called *analogy*. This reasoning pattern claims that two things that are alike in some ways will also be alike in other ways. This is the argument commonly used to justify raising the legal drinking age to 21 in all states. States in which the legal drinking age is 21 have fewer traffic deaths and fewer traffic accidents involving drunk driving. By analogy, the argument is made that if other states raised the legal drinking age to 21, drunk driving and traffic deaths would go down. Analogy says: "If it worked for you, it will work for me, too."

Once you can identify the reasoning patterns, claims, and evidence, you are well on the way to becoming a more critical listener. But there is an old saying relating to statistics that's funny but true: "Figures don't lie, but liars do figure." We can adapt that saying to another one more relevant to our purposes: "Reasoning doesn't lie, but liars do reason." In other words, what seems reasonable may not, in fact, be based on reason. There are lots of ways of making arguments that sound like they were based on reason, but actually are based on false reasoning. These are unethical appeals that resemble reasoned arguments. There are also ways of making false evidence sound like the genuine thing. In this next section we present and describe some unsound reasoning patterns and some kinds of invalid evidence and show you how to identify them so you will not be fooled.

False Reasoning and Bad Evidence

False reasoning and bad evidence can take several forms. We consider only some of the most common ones. Some false reasoning patterns are testimonials, mudslinging, bandwagon, and card-stacking. All these forms of false reasoning may take you in, if you're not careful.

Testimonials *Testimonials* are statements made by famous persons in support of something—an idea, a program, or a product. Testimonials mimic expert opinion, making it sound like the idea or program or product is supported by people whose opinions we can trust. Television advertising is probably the worst offender here, and you may have already noticed some of the silliest examples. An old ad often ridiculed is Joe Namath selling pantyhose. We might wonder what his expertise on that subject could possibly be.

Famous people often advertise products for pay. O. J. Simpson recommends rental cars; Karl Malden touts travelers checks. "Who eats corn flakes?" We hear on the television, "Does Joe Montana really eat corn flakes?" We know the athletes and movie stars get paid for such advertising, and we probably don't really believe that they use those products or that they are even experts on the kind of products they sell. Advertisers simply believe that if we associate their products with a famous name, we will remember their products better. We are smarter than that!

There are, however, more dangerous uses of testimonials that may take us in, if we are not careful. Famous people step outside their own areas of expertise to support causes and to ask us to support those causes, too. Dr. Spock was a famous and respected expert on baby and child care, but that didn't mean he was an expert on political matters. Yet he was a leader in the movement against the war in Vietnam, and many people probably listened to him because they knew and respected his name. The same political activism rebounded on Jane Fonda, who found that her reputation as a serious actress suffered from her political involvement in the antiwar movement. Sally Struthers urges us to give money to orphans overseas. What's her expertise on the subject? We have to be careful not to confuse testimonials, paid or unpaid, with expert testimony.

The best defense against being taken in by testimonials is simply to apply two simple tests. (1) What experience or credentials do they have on the subject? (2) How do they benefit from what they have said? If the people making claims have received money or other benefits from saying what they said or letting their pictures be used, we should begin to doubt their sincerity. Applying these two simple tests will make us better consumers of information and more critical listeners.

Mudslinging   Mudslinging is most often found in political campaigns. *Mudslinging* is a picturesque word for the more academic "ad hominem" argument. It simply refers to the practice of name-calling. If you can't find anything your opponent has actually done wrong, you can still call him or her names. It's a way of changing the subject from the other candidate's record (which is actually pretty good) to his or her character (which you will try to defame).

One amusing example of this political game was played out in a recent campaign for governor in Texas. The incumbent had been a good governor, and the opposition was having a hard time digging up campaign issues. The most controversial action of the incumbent was to get legislation passed that required high school athletes to maintain a certain standard in their studies or lose their eligibility to play. As a result, many popular football and basketball players weren't on the field or the court. And people were mad. Noting that the governor had never himself played on a high school team, the opponent charged: "The Governor is a Wimp!" Big headlines, and a campaign is born. Unfortunately the damage done by mudslinging is seldom amusing.

Attacking a person's character or reputation is a devious and unethical way of arguing. Too often, even when the charges are demonstrably false, the damage has been done because careless listeners have remembered and repeated or believed what was said. That is what happened during the McCarthy era; people who were accused of communism, even when they were clearly innocent, were treated as though they were in fact traitors. They lost their reputations and their employment. It's important to ask two questions about character charges when you hear them. (1) You should ask whether the charges are relevant to anything or whether they serve someone else's purpose. (2) You should demand evidence to support the charges. If the answers to these two questions aren't made to your satisfaction, you can be certain that someone is indulging in unethical mudslinging.

Bandwagon   Bandwagon appeals use social pressure to get people to change their minds. "Get on the *bandwagon,*" means to go along with the majority. It's a kind of false cause/effect reasoning. "Twenty million people can't be wrong," the advertisement argues, "so our product must be the best." More than 20 million people were wrong when they supported Hitler as Chancellor of Germany and led the world into World War II. It's more than possible for the majority to be wrong. How many people supported slavery before the Civil War? How many people bought stocks on margin in the 1920s and lost everything in the crash? How many people supported Prohibition, one of the most expensive mistakes this country ever made?

Bandwagon appeals became more dangerous with the advent in the 1940s of the opinion poll. Researchers started measuring how people felt about various social and political issues, and popularity could be documented. What was looked on before as opinion began to be viewed as quasi-scientific fact. When a majority of the people hold a certain opinion, that opinion seems to gain respectability. Presidents are now measured on their popularity instead of on their performance, which is much harder to measure.

When you hear a bandwagon appeal telling you a product is used by thousands of people or a proposition is supported by thousands of people, ask yourself why anyone would want to use that fact as an argument. What other evidence is there of the value of the product? What are the benefits of the proposal or proposition? Who benefits by your going along? If you find out that the person making the claims benefits and you don't, you want to be very skeptical of believing that public opinion is a valid measure of the truth of what that person is saying.

Card-Stacking   Card-stacking is a term borrowed from gambling, and it refers to the practice of dealing yourself the good cards and dealing your opponent the bad cards. *Card-stacking* in an argument refers to the practice of telling only the facts that support your side, even when you know that it's not the whole story. This is easy enough to do when the listeners aren't very knowledgeable about the topic, although it wouldn't work too well with an educated listener. It's usually used in arguments about complex topics like nuclear energy or the defense budget.

The Rogers Commission conclusions that pornography contributes to abusive behavior toward women have been labeled as card-stacking by people who cite important evidence that wasn't included in the report. The charge has been made that people who held contrary views weren't even asked to testify before the commission. These are serious charges, because the findings of a federal fact-finding commission may be used as evidence in court. Rapists could claim that they weren't responsible for their own behavior because they had been reading pornography. Card-stacking is another serious violation of ethical reasoning by the presentation of selected bits of evidence leading to a false conclusion.

Your best protection against card-stacking is, of course, knowledge. The more you know, the less other people can take advantage of you by lying. But the world is so complex that we can't all be educated on all issues, so the next best defense is to seek out contrary evidence when someone seems to have all the answers. When you hear a one-sided argument, ask yourself who benefits by your believing the claims. And look around to see whether there aren't equally strong arguments for the other side. By being wary and careful consumers of information, we become better critical listeners.

Ethical Persuasion

You may think by now that the world is full of traps for unwary listeners to lead them astray. You wouldn't be far wrong. W. C. Fields once said, "There's a sucker born every minute." But there are ethical people who do argue for good ideas that deserve our support. There are charities that deserve our money. There are products that are worth what they cost. In order to discover them, we need to know what to listen for. And the way to find out these good causes, ideas, and products is to ask yourself the simple Latin question *"Cui bono?"* You don't have to ask yourself in Latin, of course, so you can ask it in English, "Who benefits? Who gets something out of this?" And if the answer is that only the person asking you to believe or act benefits, you may be sure that what you are hearing is false advertising or *propaganda*. You are looking for ways in which you will benefit by believing or acting in a certain way.

An ethical persuader should be able to explain to you how you personally or the group that you belong to or the world at large will benefit by what's being offered. Some of the basic appeals that ethical persuaders have found useful follow. You can look for these appeals to judge the value or benefit of what people are claiming.

Security   You may benefit by being more secure. A good health insurance policy will make you more secure, because you will not lose all your assets as a result of a catastrophic illness. A strong national defense will make the nation more secure without costing more than we can afford to pay.

Control and Influence   You may benefit by being more in control of your own life or fate. Strong drunk driving laws have made the highways safer for all of us, because legislation took control away from the drunks and put it in the hands of the police. By voting for candidates who truly represent your viewpoint, you can get some control over the laws made in your county, state, or the nation. You can change things for the better. By managing your money wisely, you will be in more control of your own life.

Rewards   Recognition, whether it's in money, status, or public acclaim, is important to many people. Donating to a college, for example, benefits the college, but you will also benefit by being acknowledged in the alumni newsletter. Your friends will be proud of you. If you learn important listening skills, you may get a promotion before people who don't have those skills. (Could we resist putting in a plug for our own message?) Investing your money wisely will bring you financial rewards.

Feeling Good   Most of us like to be healthy, happy, and popular. Speakers may show you how you can be healthier with the right exercise and diet. Good communication skills may make you happier, because you will have more friends and you will get along at school and at work better. Learning to scuba dive or sky dive can give you hours and hours of pleasure.

Benefiting Society   Sometimes you will not benefit personally by believing or acting in a certain way, but the group you belong to or the community, state, or nation will benefit. A strong defense policy will benefit the country at large; it's hard to believe that your life will personally be spared. Still, you are probably interested in defense policy because it affects the nation as a whole.

"What do I care about day care for children of working mothers," you may ask, "I don't have any children." But nearly 80 percent of women with children are now employed, and those people (mothers and children) are an important segment of the society. We should be concerned about their welfare. While you may not personally need day care facilities, someone else in your family may. Your cousin who is divorced and has two small children needs child care. Or your sister's husband might be killed in a traffic accident. She would have to go to work, and she could use day care. Or your brother's wife could be killed, and he would need child care. Finding out how the community, state, or nation will benefit is another way of looking for ethical persuasion strategies.

Critical listening has been the subject of this chapter. You have learned what to avoid and what to look for when you're listening to persuasion. Putting that advice into practice will be the work of months and years. Only by practicing, analyzing, and evaluating your own performance will you become a better critical listener. You will not get better just by memorizing the material we have presented in this chapter. You will have to put the advice into practice. But the benefits to yourself and to the community and nation will be worth the hard work it takes to learn critical listening skills. Because we live in a country where we can and must participate in decision making to create the laws under which we live, it's our responsibility to do that logically and rationally. We should not be led by our feelings. We must use our intelligence to discover what's true and what's false, what's good and what's evil, what's possible and what's not possible. Then we must develop policies and laws based on knowledge. We should be good critical listeners.

SUMMARY

Critical listening involves listening to discover whether people are arguing from rational or emotional appeals. We pointed out that emotional arguments are often nonverbal appeals, using images or music to create a mood or feeling. There are also verbal emotional appeals that include appeals to patriotism, to pride, to fear, to elitism, to faddism, and to guilt. Making decisions on the basis of feelings or moods is dangerous because it bypasses the reasoning process. You may be fooled into believing something that's false or into acting against your own best interest by listening to emotional appeals.

The best way to discover what you should believe is to look for rational arguments. We showed you how to identify rational appeals and valid arguments. We pointed out that rational appeals involve three parts: claims, arguments, and evidence. We described three kinds of evidence and explained how to evaluate the validity of expert opinion and research results. We also identified four common reasoning patterns that are used to connect evidence with claims: cause/effect, induction, deduction, and analogy. The false reasoning and evidence you may run into include testimonials, bandwagon appeals, card-stacking, and mudslinging. These practices resemble rational argument, but they are false. Ethical speakers will avoid the use of emotional appeals and will present evidence to show that their ideas will benefit you or your social group by providing security, control and influence, rewards, good feelings, or a significant benefit to society.

Critical listening is clearly not a simple process, but one that will take you much effort to master. It's vital for citizens in a democracy to be good critical listeners, because they shape the social world in which they live.

SUGGESTED ACTIVITIES

1. Read the editorial pages in your local paper. Identify whether the editorials use emotional appeals or rational appeals. What reasoning patterns are used? What evidence is presented to support rational claims?

2. Read the letters to the editor in your local paper. Identify whether those letter writers use emotional or rational appeals. What reasoning patterns are used? What evidence is presented in support of claims? Are the claims valid?

3. Collect magazine advertisements for different kinds of products. Analyze the appeals used in the advertisements: Are they rational or emotional appeals? What evidence is used to support claims?

4. Test your understanding of the concepts of fact, inference, and judgment by identifying which of the following statements are facts, which are inferences, and which are judgments:

_____ Phyllis isn't going to last long at this job.

_____ Phyllis has clocked in late every day this week.

_____ Phyllis is lazy and incompetent.

_____ Nylon makes the best tents.

_____ Nylon tents will not leak in the rain.

_____ My nylon tent did not leak when it rained.

_____ Jerry is a juvenile delinquent.

_____ Jerry was convicted of shoplifting.

_____ Jerry is going to end up in jail.

5. Test your understanding of the qualifications for expert witnesses on some examples. Which of the following statements should be accepted as testimony of a qualified expert?

_____ Medical doctors recommend aspirin for this condition.

_____ A nationally prominent physician recommends aspirin for pain.

_____ A medical researcher from the Hershey Medical Center recommends aspirin for relief of pain.

_____ Dr. J. L. Richards, head of internal medicine at the Hershey Medical Center, recommends aspirin for relief of pain. Dr. Richards has recently been elected to membership in the College of Medical Surgeons.

6. To test your understanding of these common reasoning patterns, see if you can identify the reasoning behind these claims:

_____ Northern Amalgamated has a flextime program and it works very well
for them. We should try it here.

_____ When I let my employees come in
half an hour early and leave early,
our work group increased its production by 3 percent. I think flextime
is a good idea.

_____ Studies have shown that workers
who feel they have some say in their
work conditions produce better; I
think flextime should be instituted in
our company.

_____ If we institute a flextime program so
people could work at their own con-
venience, we could increase production and reduce absenteeism.

7. Try creating your own rational arguments using the four patterns of
reasoning outlined in the text. Take a topic from current affairs in your community or in the nation and see how you might make arguments both for and against
a specific proposal using cause/effect, induction, deduction, and analogy as reasoning patterns. What types of evidence could you use for each of these arguments?

REFERENCES AND RECOMMENDED READING

Beardsley, Monroe. *Thinking Straight.* Englewood Cliffs, NJ: Prentice-Hall, 1979.

Borisoff, Deborah, and Lisa Merrill. *The Power to Communicate.* Prospect Heights IL:
Waveland Press, 1985.

Bradley, Bert. *Credibility of Ideas* (4th Edition). Dubuque, IA: William C. Brown, 1984.

Hayakawa, S. I. *Language in Thought and Action* (4th Edition). New York: Harcourt
Brace Jovanovich, 1978.

Mehrabian, Albert. *Silent Messages.* Belmont, CA: Wadsworth, 1971.

Newman, E. *Strictly Speaking.* Indianapolis, IN: Bobbs-Merrill, 1974.

Postman, N. *Crazy Talk, Stupid Talk.* New York: Delacorte Press, 1976.

Shrope, Wayne Austin. *Speaking and Listening.* New York: Harcourt Brace Jovanovich,
1979.

Willard, Charles A. *Argumentation and the Social Grounds of Knowledge.* Tuscaloosa, AL:
The University of Alabama Press, 1983.

Wilson, Gerald L., Alan M. Hantz, and Michael S. Hanna. *Interpersonal Growth Through
Communication.* Dubuque, IA: William C. Brown, 1985.

chapter 7

Listening to Enjoy

When you have finished reading this chapter you should be able to:

1. Identify and describe three levels of listening to enjoy.
2. Describe how we enjoy music and oral literature physically, on the level of sensation.
3. Explain how to learn to listen on the physical level.
4. Describe how we enjoy music and oral literature mentally, on the level of ideas.
5. Explain how to learn to listen on the level of ideas.
6. Describe how we enjoy music and oral literature on the level of technical expertise.
7. Explain how to learn to listen on the level of technical expertise.

When you have finished reading this chapter you should be able to define these terms:

1. oral literature
2. rhythm, melody, harmony
3. syncopation
4. rhyme
5. imagery
6. theme, character, plot
7. program music
8. music theory
9. form

10. absolute music
11. symbolism
12. musicality

How in the world could we write a whole chapter about listening to enjoy? After all, what's there to learn about listening to enjoy? You either like it or you don't. Maybe you feel like the guy in the art museum who said he didn't know anything about art, but he knew what he liked. Telling people they should be interested in modern art or classical music or opera (or country music or pop art or Gilbert and Sullivan) will not lead them to seek out and enjoy new things. Telling people what they should do has always been singularly ineffective. There is nothing that turns you off something quite so quickly as having someone tell you you should be interested in it. Right away it's the last thing you want to do. So we will not tell you to change what you like. Instead, we will tell you how to enjoy more what you already like. And maybe you will be led to ask questions about what else you might learn to like if you had the opportunity. It's up to you.

This chapter on listening to enjoy will focus mostly on art: music, poetry, and plays. All cultures have art in various forms: music, painting, sculpture, poetry, storytelling. Creating art seems to be a distinctively human activity and one that's very important to both our personal well-being and to the health and viability of the culture. Art mirrors, expresses, and interprets our lives and gives us meaning. It's a way of sharing experience and creating a sense of community.

LISTENING TO MUSIC AND LITERATURE

Since this is a book about listening, we focus on the arts that involve sound and listening: music and literature. In the last century and in the first part of this century, speechmaking was also considered an art, and people traveled miles to hear speeches. Even political speeches. But times have changed, and political speeches now serve as a context for the 30-second cut that will appear on the nightly television news. Making speeches has fallen into disrepute as an art form, and people seldom look forward to them as interesting social occasions. Many people have come to distrust people who speak well, and a certain ineptness is often looked on as evidence of sincerity. So although people who give speeches and people who study speeches might enjoy hearing good speeches, we will not treat speechmaking as a serious art form for the purposes of this book. But everything we say about music and poetry and plays can equally well be applied to speechmaking and, yes, to conversation, too. Before radio and television, people used to spend whole evenings talking to one another. Conversation can be carried to an art form, if you want to invest the time and thought to the subject.

> I have my great-grandmother's journal from the years 1893 to 1896. She lived on a farm in Kansas, and she wrote down everything she did each day. She spent a lot of time baking and sewing, I can tell you. But one entry is really fascinating. The whole family took the train to Hutchinson, a two-hour trip, to hear the speeches. And then took the train home again. Just to hear speeches?

I can imagine how hot it was in July, and the dust! To listen to speeches all day? When speakers come on the television, I turn them off. How different our lives are, hers and mine.

Three Levels of Listening to Enjoy

In this chapter we have arranged the topic of listening to enjoy into three main sections. These three sections are based on ideas developed by Aaron Copland (1960) about the appreciation of music. Copland pointed out that people can enjoy music on three different levels. On the first level, they can enjoy the aspects of music that affect them physically: rhythm, tone, harmony, melody. People can tap their feet or snap their fingers or hum along with the music. They can dance. This physical enjoyment of music is an important element of enjoyment, although it's on a very basic physical level of appreciation.

Copland's second level of music enjoyment focuses on the ideas that can be found in music. Music can remind us of other things, of other times and places, and of feelings and sensations that aren't physically present when we are listening to the music. For example, music can remind us of birds singing or can imitate the sound of wind in the pine trees. Music can express the rhythms of our lives, the hustle and bustle and traffic in the city. Music can express emotions—gaiety, sorrow, terror, rage, loneliness. Music can also be used to tell stories as in ballads and operas. In all these ways music has the capacity to take us outside ourselves and give us vicarious experience of the world. We can also enjoy music on this second, ideational level.

The final level of musical enjoyment that Copland talked about was what he called musicality. People who know the technical aspects of the music—who understand both the theory and the practice of making music—can enjoy music on another level entirely. They can appreciate the technical expertise that goes into a piece of music to create the effects we hear. Someone who's trained in music will know what a piece of music would sound like from reading the score. Not only can they recognize the composer, they can also recognize the artist who's interpreting the music. The expert can understand why the composer chose just those notes and no others and how the different instruments or voices work together to produce just that effect. To understand music on this level requires years of training, and it requires that you learn a whole new vocabulary to talk about the music. This is a level of appreciation that isn't open to all of us. But it's also a valuable way of appreciating music.

In this chapter we apply Copland's category scheme to the appreciation not only of music, but also of literature that's presented orally. *Oral literature* usually means plays and poetry, although any piece of literature can be read aloud for enjoyment. We want to make it clear that none of these levels of enjoyment of either music or poetry and plays is necessarily any better or higher or more important than another. They coexist, and you can choose to take advantage of any of them as you please. Understanding the technical mastery of the music doesn't prevent you from enjoying the physical sensations of rhythm and harmony. It simply gives you a choice of levels on which to enjoy what you're listening to.

Karl Haas, a world famous expert on music, explains in his book *Inside Music* that when he was a student of music, he would go to each concert twice. During the first performance, he would sit with the score in his lap, studying what the orchestra and the soloists were doing and learning as much as he could about the music. Then during the second performance, he would just sit and listen to the music to enjoy it. In other words, for the first hearing Mr. Haas set himself a goal to listen on the third level—musicality—and for the second hearing he set himself a goal to listen for ideas, the second level we will consider. By learning to listen on different levels, you too can increase your understanding and enjoyment not only of music, but of all oral performances.

ENJOYMENT ON THE PHYSICAL LEVEL

Listening for enjoyment on the physical level seems a natural process. Even small babies enjoy rhythmic patterns as they sway and clap to music. The physical appreciation of music and language is a response to certain aspects of both that affect us without our having to think about it. Rhythm, melody, and harmony are important aspects of music that we appreciate without much training.

Rhythm

Rhythm is a basic and an important element of music. *Rhythm* creates the movement of the music; it's almost impossible not to respond to the beat. We are surrounded by a great variety of rhythms in the music we listen to. We have marching rhythms that are suitable for ceremonial occasions: graduations, weddings, funerals. We have dance rhythms in a wide variety of forms from square dancing to waltzes to rock and roll. We have Latin rhythms like the tango, calypso, and reggae.

You're probably most familiar with the commonest rhythm in western music which has a weak beat following a strong beat: da duh, da duh, da duh, da duh. This is the 4/4 beat of ballads and folk songs, and it's also the basic rhythm of speech in the English language:

> As I was going to St. Ives,
> I met a man with seven wives,
> And seven wives had seven sacks,
> And seven bags had seven cats,
> And seven cats had seven kits,
> Kits, cats, sacks, wives,
> How many were going to St Ives?

Chopin's "Funeral March" is a good example of that kind of rhythm used in a solemn, stately way. Most country and western music and folk songs like ballads use this pattern of rhythm. But turn that rhythm around and you get syncopation, which is a common rhythm in jazz. *Syncopation* puts the strong beat first, followed by a weak beat. Syncopation gives music an upbeat, gay, and lively feeling. Gershwin's tunes "I Got Rhythm" and "Fascinating Rhythm" are good examples of the use of syncopated rhythm. Rhythm and blues and rock and roll both use syncopation to produce their effects. "Shake, Rattle, and Roll" and "Rock Around the Clock" are examples of syncopation. A 3/4 beat rhythm gives us waltzes and the polka, which are graceful and lively dance rhythms. It's hard to resist tapping your feet or moving your body to the music when you hear the "Blue Danube Waltz," "The Skater's Waltz," or the "Beer Barrel Polka."

Rhythm is also an important element in poetry. Carefully chosen and controlled rhythmic patterns are one distinguishing mark of poetry. Modern poetry often mimics the conversational rhythms of everyday speech, so we don't notice the rhythm as a strong element. But poetry of earlier times was strongly rhythmic. Early epic poems which were used to relate the history of a particular people were written with a strong and regular beat. By putting the poem into a repetitious rhythmic pattern, the bards who recited the long poems could remember them more easily. Between the time of the bards of ancient Greece and Ireland and the present, our poets have experimented with a wide variety of rhythms.

We have, for example, the classic ballad form of four lines of equal length rhyming. This example is from a Robin Hood ballad:

> There are twelve months in all the year
>   As I hear many men say,
> But the merriest month in all the year
>   Is the merry month of May.

This form is nice for telling stories. It moves along smoothly and lets you think about what you are hearing. If you listen to the first stanza of this early English ballad, you can hear that it was meant to be sung:

> Come lasses and lads, take leave of your dads,
>   And away to the Maypole hey;
> For every he has got a she
>   With a Minstrel standing by:
>   For Willy has gotten his Jill,
>   And Johnny has got his Joan,
> To jig it, jig it, jig it, jig it, jig it up and down.

Reading that verse aloud you can hear where some words would be held longer and some sung faster to make the rhythm come out right for dancing.

Later poets experimented with blank verse that had lines of equal length but no rhyme. Shakespeare was a master of blank verse as the following example from *The Tempest* will illustrate. In this excerpt Prospero is explaining to Ferdinand and Miranda that the visions they have just seen were magic:

> These our actors,
> As I foretold you, were all spirits and
> Are melted into air, into thin air:
> And, like the baseless fabric of this vision,

The cloud-capped towers, the gorgeous palaces,
The solemn temples, the great globe itself,
Yea, all which it inherit, shall dissolve
And, like this insubstantial pageant faded,
Leave not a rack behind. We are such stuff
As dreams are made on, and our little life
Is rounded with a sleep.

If you read this poetry for its meaning, the rhythm will take care of itself. The rhythm is much more complex and subtle than the simple da duh, da duh of the rhymed ballads that preceded it.

Modern poets, starting with the English romantic poets, have begun using conversational rhythms in their poetry to make the poetry more accessible to common readers. Taking the sounds of everyday speech, they refine the rhythms into poetry as in this excerpt from a poem by John Ciardi about a little boy named Benn:

Look outside. Do you see Small Benn
Digging a cave to be his den?
He doesn't want to live with us.
He says he's tired of Mummy's fuss.
He says he's tired of Daddy's ways
Of being *reasonable*. He says
Daddy's reasons are much too long
And they always end with *Benn is wrong.*

Rhythm is a basic element, if not the basic element, of physical pleasure in both music and poetry. Whether it's simple or complex, we respond to rhythm in both poetry and music.

Rhyme

Rhyme is another common poetic technique that gives us physical pleasure. The repetition of sounds at the ends of phrases creates a musical quality and gives us a feeling of completion. Used as a memory device to help the bards remember long passages of stories and histories, rhyme is an important element of many songs. We have already seen how rhyming every other line is a common technique in songs, especially ballads. Couplets, lines rhymed two by two, give a choppy feeling that lends itself well to humor. This is an excerpt from a poem by Lew Sarett called "Hollyhocks":

I have a garden, but, oh, dear me!
What a ribald and hysterical company:
Incorrigible mustard, militant corn,
Frivolous lettuce, and celery forlorn;
Beets apoplectic and fatuous potatoes,
Voluptuous pumpkins and palpitant tomatoes;

And there are more complex rhyming schemes that also give us pleasure and work to tie the ideas of the poem together. John Donne wrote some very passionate love poems in complicated rhyme schemes as illustrated in this passage from one of his most famous poems, "The Canonization":

> For God's sake hold your tongue, and let me love;
> Or chide my palsy, or my gout;
> My five gray hairs, or ruined fortune flout;
> With wealth your state, your mind with arts improve;
>   Take you a course, get you a place,
>   Observe his Honor, or his Grace;
> Or the king's real, or his stamped face
> Contemplate; what you will, approve,
> So you will let me love.

Some poets seem in love with the sound of words, without paying much attention to the meaning. They play with words, stringing together different sounds and textures to create a complex pattern in much the same way impressionist painters seem to slop colors together to create an effect. Gerard Manley Hopkins was such a poet. This is the first stanza of a poem he called "The Leaden Echo":

> How to keep—is there any, any, is there none such, nowhere known,
>   some bow or brooch or brain or brace, lace, latch or catch or
>   key to keep
> Back beauty, keep it, beauty, beauty, beauty, . . . from vanishing
>   away?
> Oh, is there no frowning of these wrinkles, ranked wrinkles deep,
> Down? no waving-off of these most mournful messengers, still mes-
>   sengers, sad and stealing messengers of gray?
> No, there's none, there's none—oh, no, there's none!
> Nor can you long be, what you now are, called fair—
> Do what you may, do what you may,
> And wisdom is early to despair:

What in the world is he talking about? Well, actually this is a very common theme of romantic poetry: Beauty doesn't last. But you have to read very hard to figure it out. Instead of attending to the sense of the poetry, notice what Hopkins does with the sounds of the words. Notice especially in the second line how he plays with the sounds of "b" in "bow or brooch or brain or brace" and then shifts attention to the last sounds in "brace, lace, latch or catch." Notice also the shifted patterns in the vowels in that line from "bow-broach" to "brain-brace-lace" to "latch-catch." This is a master of language, making music of sound in poetry.

We still occasionally hear poetry in speechmaking. Martin Luther King, Jr. was a well-known user of the poetic style in his speechmaking. He used rhythm, melody, and rhyme to give shape to his speeches. His "I Have a Dream" speech is often used an an example to illustrate the importance of musical and poetic elements in persuasive speaking. The physical effect of his speeches on his audience is well documented. King moved audiences to believe in his message and to act with him in peaceful demonstrations for civil rights.

In plays, our other main form of oral literature, physical appreciation often focuses on visual elements: the setting, the costumes, the movement. Listening appreciation on the physical level would mostly apply to the music that might accompany the play. Operas and musical comedy are the two most popular forms of oral literature that rely on musical elements for their effect. Some of the most popular operas you may have heard of, even if you aren't a great fan of opera, are *Rigoletto, La Traviata, Aida, Carmen,* and *La Boheme. The King and I* was recently revived on Broadway and played to packed audiences. *Oklahoma, South Pacific, Carousel,* and *My Fair Lady* are only a few of the famous musical plays of that time. More recently the rock musicals *Tommy* and *Hair* combined music and drama.

Melody and Harmony

Melody and *harmony* are two more elements of music that can elicit a purely physical response. You don't have to understand or read music to enjoy songs. The interplay of rhythm and harmony in spirituals, gospel music, and barbershop quartet songs are accessible to listeners of all ages and stages of musical sophistication. We show our appreciation of melody and harmony by singing along, whistling, or humming the tune.

How to Enjoy on the Physical Level

In our modern lives literature has become something we read silently, not something we read aloud and share. When is the last time you and your friends spent an afternoon or an evening reading a play aloud or reading poetry to one another? Instead of participating in literature, we have become passive observers of literature. We go to the movies or we rent videos. We watch television. We don't *do* literature any more, we *watch* it. If you read poetry at all, you probably read it silently by yourself.

By turning the enjoyment of literature into a passive and silent affair, we have lost some of the elements that made both poetry and plays an important and enjoyable physical experience. We no longer hear the rhythms or the melody of a line of poetry. We don't appreciate the sounds of the language we speak. Language has become a basis of exchange of information, rather like money is the basis of exchange of goods. It seems to have lost its power to move and delight us, even on a physical level.

To enjoy music or literature on a physical level, you actually have to hear it. You have to go to where the music is or you have to participate yourself. You can listen to music on the radio or on records or cassettes. But to experience the music fully, you should attend a concert. Enjoying the music in company with other people makes the experience more exciting. Participation in music making is also open to most people. Most communities have amateur music groups in all kinds and sizes. You can sing in choirs or barbershop ensembles. You can play instrumental music in Renaissance groups, orchestras, jazz groups, bands, or chamber music groups. Participation in music will increase your understanding and enjoyment of the physical aspects of the music, while at the same time you will be learning more about music. You will also be learning to appreciate music on other levels—on the levels of ideas and of technical mastery.

Participation in oral literature is also available in most communities. If you don't feel like acting in a local theater group, you can attend performances. Even if the performance isn't quite up to professional standards, often the beauty of the language will shine through. And professional companies tour regularly, giving you the opportunity to see excellent productions of many popular and classic pieces of literature. To enjoy both music and literature on a physical level, you need to participate. You have to become an active, rather than a passive, participant.

ENJOYMENT ON THE LEVEL OF IDEAS

Copland's second level of musical appreciation was an appreciation of ideas contained in the music. You might like music because it reminds you of a particular place or event. Or the music may tell a story. You enjoy and remember literature because it has an important message for your life. This is a mental, instead of a physical, appreciation of literature or music. We begin with the appreciation of literature, because you may be more familiar with thinking of plays or poetry as conveying ideas. We discuss plays and poetry, and then we look for how ideas are expressed in music.

Dramatic Elements

When you attend a play, you will be aware of certain elements of the play that carry the meaning. There are plot, character, and theme or the elements of the play that are symbolic. The plot contains the action of the play. Something is happening. Usually there is a situation in which there is some conflict, the conflict comes to a climax, and there is a resolution of the conflict. The *characters* in the play are especially important, since the whole play moves through what they say and do. There is no description in a play, as there is in novels or poetry; we can only know what the actors can tell us or show us. So understanding the characters is especially important to our enjoyment of plays. Finally there is the *theme,* which refers to the ideas around which the play is built. A play has to be *about* something; it can't just be a slice of daily life. The theme contains the meaning of the play. We explore each of these elements in this section.

Plot   The *plot* of the play is a summary of the actual events that take place on the stage. Sometimes the plot is important to the play, but sometimes it takes second or even third place to the characters or to the general theme of the play. If we describe the plot of *Hamlet* you will think it must be the most boring and silly story ever told. In *Hamlet* a young prince of Denmark learns that his uncle has killed his father and married his mother, and Hamlet has to figure out what to do about it. Finally he gets in a fight and dies. Actually, nearly everybody dies in the end. How could such a tale have held the attention of generations of playgoers? The plot is only the skeleton on which the rest of the play hangs. You couldn't tell much about a person's personality, beauty, virtue, wit, or grace by looking at a skeleton. So the plot of the play may only serve as a medium for the playwright to tell his real story.

Theme   The themes in *Hamlet* are what have held the attention of theater goers for centuries. These themes are complex and open to many interpretations. Shakespeare used this play to examine the nature of kingship, and the relationship between the ruler's virtue and the general welfare of the nation. By custom and law, Hamlet was bound to revenge his father's death by killing his uncle, but he delayed that revenge. Instead, he soliloquized over his dilemma, posing action against inaction, considering the consequences. Shakespeare added still another dimension to the play by putting a play within a play, as strolling minstrels act out the real king's murder before Hamlet's uncle (now the king) and his court. The play makes us feel we are all players on the stage of life, and we question the parts that are written for us. Like Hamlet we are all faced with dilemmas of what we should do and what we wish to do. We question our actions: Are they right or wrong? It's the ideas in Hamlet that are important, not the plot.

Character   Character is another important representational element in litera-ture, and much of the enjoyment of plays and poetry is in appreciation of the characters who take part in the action. Some characters even take on a life of their own and step outside the particular poem or play to become a part of the culture. Shakespeare was a master of characterization, and many of his characters have become part of the common culture of people who have never read or seen his plays. Romeo and Juliet have become symbolic of young lovers, and we have all heard of Falstaff and Shylock. From other famous works of literature Don Quixote and his faithful Sancho are such characters as are Joan of Arc and Cleopatra. Characters in a play are not just individuals, playing out their own lives on the stage; they represent types that we can identify with and understand. So Willy Loman in *Death of a Salesman* is in some way all men, and *Our Town* really is every little town in the United States. By vicarious experience through the characters in a play, we can enlarge our own understanding of the world and gain new insight and wisdom.

Symbolism   Often literature is used as a vehicle for social ideas. Plays can use character and plot to explore a situation and possible solutions for important social problems. The Russian playwright Anton Chekhov wrote plays about Russian society; one of the most famous is *The Cherry Orchard. A Raisin in the Sun* is a contemporary play that explores the situation of a black urban family in the United States. Charles Dickens created masterful descriptions of charac-ters and situations of urban life in nineteenth-century England, and his stories contained commentary on many social issues relating to the effects of the Industrial Revolution on people's lives. Some of his stories have been presented on the stage, most notably *A Christmas Carol* and *Nicholas Nickelby.* The musical comedy *South Pacific* deals with the themes of war and racial prejudice during World War II.

Poetic Elements

While plot, theme, and character are important elements of some poetry, we are probably more aware of imagery as an integral aspect of poetry. *Imagery* is the use of words to evoke a picture, a sound, a smell, a taste, or a feeling. Some imagery evokes ideas. A Japanese haiku poem is a small poem intended simply to present a single image for our enjoyment and contemplation. Here's a haiku poem by Basho:

> White cherry blossoms;
> white wisp of mist;
> dawn-lit mountains.

And here's another miniature image written by Issa:

> The old, plump bullfrog
> held his ground and stared at me—
> what a sour face!

Haiku is a Japanese form of poetry, but images are also an important part of our Western poetry. Images function to elicit responses from us on lots of different levels. We may associate the images with events in our past, with events we have heard of, with experiences we have had, with ideas or imaginings that bear no relationship to the real world. Or images may only paint a more vivid picture of things we see every day and neglect to notice.

As a final example of how images are used to evoke and portray ideas, we take a poem from the romantic poets. William Wordsworth was a master of using images to catch his meaning. Here's his sonnet called "To Sleep":

> A flock of sheep that leisurely pass by,
> One after one; the sound of rain and bees
> Murmuring; the fall of rivers, winds and seas,
> Smooth fields, white sheets of water, a, .d pure sky:
> I've thought of all by turns, and yet do lie
> Sleepless! and soon the small birds' melodies
> Must hear, first utter'd from my orchard trees,
> And the first cuckoo's melancholy cry.
> Even thus last night, and two nights more I lay,
> And could not win thee, Sleep! by any stealth:
> So do not let me wear to-night away:

Without Thee what is all the morning's wealth?
Come, blessed barrier between day and day
Dear mother of fresh thoughts and joyous health!

Anyone who has spent a sleepless night must understand what Wordsworth was saying. But the poet said it so much better than you or I could. By saying it so well, he took an ordinary experience and turned it into art for our contemplation and enjoyment. Appreciating the ideas that occur to you as you experience art is the second level that Copland was talking about.

Program Music

From literature, we turn to music to look for ideas in art. Music that's written with an underlying plot or story is called *program music.* Program music includes anthems, cantatas, chorales, songs, operas and oratorios, overtures, and symphonic or tone poems. This is a very broad category of music and includes music from many different periods and countries. Anthems were a particularly British kind of music, but eventually became popularized in the national anthems we are familiar with today. You are probably most familiar with cantatas as religious music, associated with celebrations at Christmas or Easter. Cantatas are vocal music that usually tell stories or celebrate particular occasions.

A lot of program music includes parts for the voice, allowing for storytelling and plot and characterization. The most dramatic music of this kind is probably opera. There are operas in all languages; you have probably heard of *The Barber of Seville, Tosca, Carmen, La Boheme, La Traviata, Aida, Boris Godunov,* and *Porgy and Bess.* Operas can be comic or tragic, historical, mythological, or romantic. There are operas for every taste and occasion. Handel's oratorios are probably the most famous, and they are often performed today. Everyone must have heard parts of Handel's *Messiah* performed regularly at Christmas and Easter.

Another way we can appreciate music on this representational level is to listen to music that develops a theme. Symphonic or tone poems are instrumental music that captures the spirit of poems, historical incidents, geographic scenes, or natural phenomena. Mussorgsky's *Pictures at an Exhibition* is a popular example of the genre. Respighi wrote three pieces to describe Rome: *The Fountains of Rome, The Pines of Rome,* and *Roman Festivals.* Walt Disney made Dukas' *The Sorcerer's Apprentice* into his famous movie *Fantasia.*

So we see that all the same elements of theme, plot, and character are available in music, too. Some composers have made story elements central to their orchestral compositions. You are probably familiar with Tchaikovsky's *Peter and the Wolf,* the Russian fairy tale set to music. Tchaikovsky also wrote more serious music that contained plot elements, notably the *1812 Overture* telling the story of the defeat of Napoleon by the Russians. In this composition the music mirrors the battle action, and the score includes both French and Russian national anthems and the sound of a real cannon in the last part of the piece.

Folk music contains story elements on a more personal level than the formal compositions of great composers. Folk music, like folk stories, deals most often with elements of love, death, and work. "Frankie and Johnnie" is a typical folk song of love gone wrong, and "Barbara Allen" is another example. Spirituals like "Go Down, Moses" and "All God's Chillun Got Shoes" express the feelings of the slaves. "Old Dan Tucker" and "Camptown Races" tell stories of the South; "Sweet Betsy from Pike" tells the story of a pioneer woman. Many elements of folk music can be found in the popular music of today, particularly in bluegrass and country and western music.

How to Enjoy on the Level of Ideas

To appreciate literature or music on the representational level, we have to study the subject a little. Literature and music appreciation courses are a good way to start understanding such elements as plot, theme, character, and symbolism. You are probably already familiar with the basic concepts from your high school classes. Most universities offer courses in theater or in oral interpretation of literature that can introduce you to aspects of literature that you had not been aware of before.

You can also acquire knowledge about the literature or music you're interested in by talking to people with similar interests and by reading about them in magazines and books. There are clubs and associations devoted to the study of almost any topic, from science fiction to classical music. "Star Trek" fans, calling themselves "Trekkies," have annual conventions, and most large communities will have at least one opera society or chamber music society. Look through the magazine selections at your local book store or in the local library. You will find specialized magazines devoted to almost every kind of interest you could imagine.

Radio stations usually specialize in one type of music, and the programming may include shows discussing the music. The public radio network features music of all kinds, and it also features talk shows devoted to playing and discussing most types of music. For example, on the local station on Saturday afternoons, there is a half-hour program devoted solely to Celtic music from Scotland, Wales, and Ireland. The woman who hosts the show plays music and talks about the musical traditions and the artists who are playing the music. There are also programs devoted to chamber music, bluegrass, and other types of music that are out of the mainstream music played on commercial radio stations.

When you listen to enjoy the ideas in music or literature, you listen for different things from what you listen for to enjoy the physical sensations. You will be listening to understand the ideas that are presented in the music or on the stage. Your role will be a more passive than an active one. When you listen to enjoy the ideas you should let your mind wander and see what associations you find with the music or the words you're hearing. What do they remind you of? What feelings do they call to mind? What experiences do you remember when you hear a certain piece of music or see a scene from a play? What memories does the poem call to your mind? By examining the various associations that the art conjures up in your mind, you can expand your own awareness of the world around you.

Your mind is a vast network of associated ideas, feelings, thoughts, attitudes, values, and sensations. As you build more connections between and among ideas, you will be able to learn and understand more things, whether or not musical. You have often heard people say "You should listen with an open mind." Listening to understand and enjoy the ideas you hear is one important way of listening with an open mind.

ENJOYMENT ON THE LEVEL OF MUSICALITY OR TECHNICAL EXPERTISE

Learning to listen to enjoy literature or music on the level of technical expertise remains an option for people who are willing to spend a good deal of time studying the topic. In this section we illustrate how such expert knowledge can make listening more enjoyable. We also indicate some ways you can go about getting technical and expert knowledge of literature and music.

We begin with Copland's own field of expertise—music. Musicality or the technical mastery of music includes understanding of both *music theory* and musical practice. That is, you need to know how music is written to produce specific effects as well as how to play different instruments. It would also help to have some knowledge of the history of music and some knowledge of different musical traditions. Understanding music from different times and places can help us understand our own music better. You can see that the area of study is vast; it would take a lifetime to understand music completely. Fortunately, such a complete understanding isn't necessary for us to begin to learn to listen on the level of musicality.

Let's begin with some basic ideas about music theory and see how they can add to our understanding of and appreciation for music. Karl Haas tells us that music is made up of rhythm, melody, harmony, tonal color, and form. If we want to understand how music works, we have to understand these concepts. We have already considered some of these ideas, so let's look at the idea of form. In his book *Inside Music* Haas explains how form is tied to the ideas of symmetry and regularity, along with contrast and change. In music, *form* refers to the patterns of sound we hear when we listen. Notes follow one another in a pattern that repeats itself or in variations of that pattern. Form can be simple or elaborate. Form is particularly important to music that doesn't have plot or ideas as part of its appeal; this kind of music is called *absolute music* to distinguish it from the program music we considered in the previous section of this chapter.

Absolute Music

The forms of absolute music with which we are most familiar are the sonata, concerto, symphony, chamber music, and counterpoint. This music is instrumental; there are no words. The music doesn't represent anything but itself, so an understanding of its technical structure is important to its appreciation. For example, the sonata is written for individual instruments, either alone or in combination. Sonatas don't have names; they are given numbers or are designated by the instruments for which they are written. Some of Beethoven's better known sonatas include Sonata No. 9 for Violin and Piano, Sonata No. 23 for Piano, and his Trio No. 6 for Violin, Cello, and Piano. It would be silly to ask what these sonatas are about; they are about music—what the instruments can do.

Musical Form   As an example of classical musical form, let's consider the sonata. Sonatas are composed of different parts called movements; each movement usually has three parts: exposition, development, and recapitulation. A musical theme or melody will be stated in the exposition; there will be variations of that theme in the development; the movement will end with a recapitulation of the original theme or melody. There are usually three movements in a sonata; the second movement is traditionally slower than the first, and the final movement is traditionally livelier. When you understand the structure of a sonata, you will be able to listen for and identify the various movements, themes, and variations that produce the completed work of art. Then when you listen to a sonata it will not just sound like a long passage of notes that keep sort of repeating themselves. Although the form of a sonata is traditional, each sonata is unique because of the many variations that are possible within the traditional form. Like no two snowflakes are alike, no two sonatas are alike. If you get the idea that absolute music bears a resemblance to mathematics you aren't far wrong; both are abstract kinds of art that are best appreciated by people who study them deeply.

Jazz also has form, but jazz form is very different from classical form. In classical music, regularity is important; the aim is to recreate exactly what the composer intended. In jazz the form is fluid and flexible. Jazz musicians compose as they play. They take a song and interpret that song in their performances, so each jazz artist has a particular style that's recognizable as a musical signature. Maybe you're familiar with names like Dizzy Gillespie, Bessie Smith, Miles Davis, Count Basie, Duke Ellington, and Dave Brubeck. The same song played by each of these artists would sound very different. Music buffs can recognize each jazz artist, as classical music buffs can recognize particular compositions.

A lot of jazz takes the form of call-and-response, with two solo instruments answering one another. But in jazz the form isn't nearly as important as the style. The instruments in jazz attempt to recreate the human voice, so they focus on the effect instead of the form. Notes often fall between the cracks of the traditional scales or wail or glide to express the emotions of the player and the song.

Musical Instruments

Knowing something about the instrument or instruments for which the sonata was written would also add to your enjoyment of music. We can take the piano as an example, since a great deal of sonata music has been written for the piano. The piano is a keyboard instrument, which gives it certain limitations as well as certain advantages. In a piano the sound is produced by wooden hammers hitting strings inside a case with a sounding board. This construction differentiates the piano from string instruments, which are played with a bow (violin) or plucked (harp), as well as from percussion instruments like the drum and cymbals. Some great advantages of the piano as an instrument are its range of notes (from very low to very high), its range of expression (from very soft to very loud), and the ability of the player to use harmony (striking several notes at one time). Most pianos also have two pedals which allow the pianist to soften the tone and to sustain the notes. A composition written for harpsichord, another keyboard instrument, would have to be more limited in range and expression. The harpsichord has no pedals, so notes can't be sustained, and harmony is created more often by runs and arpeggios.

The European tradition of classical music aims for regularity of pitch, timbre, and vibrato; there is a particular "right" way for a piano, a French horn, or a violin to sound. Not so in jazz, where the performer is aiming for an individual effect. Jazz instrumentalists vary the vibrato, veil the timbre, slide their notes, and use tremolo and overtones to produce distinctive styles. There was only one Louis Armstrong, because he was the only one who played the trumpet in that inimitable style. Jazz players have used all kinds of things as "mutes" to get different sounds from their instruments: tomato cans, silk stockings, a felt hat, and even the "plumber's helper." Innovation is the name of the game in jazz.

Jazz rhythm is much more complex than classical rhythm. It stems from the African rhythms that Western musicians are only beginning to understand. It's nothing special for an African drummer to keep eight separate rhythmic patterns going in the same performance, a complexity that mystifies American ears. One writer noted that a master African drummer would find most American jazz rhythms child's play, like comparing tic-tac-toe to chess. The more you know about jazz, the more interesting it becomes.

Background and History of the Music

It's becoming pretty clear that there is a good deal to learn about music if you want to learn to understand it on the level of technical expertise. In addition to knowing something about the form and the instrument, you will also gain more appreciation for music by knowing about the composer, the styles of the time, and the relationship of the music to the lives of the people who lived then. Music has a history, and understanding how the technical development of instruments affected the compositions can help you understand particular pieces of music. Sometimes understanding the political and economic conditions of the time are important to an understanding of music. If you have seen the movie *Amadeus* you will know that composers of those days were employed by rich and important people for their own entertainment. That's rather a different situation from today! Remember the great debate in the movie over whether Mozart's opera should be written in Italian or German? That was an important debate as nationalism came to be a strong force in the Europe of Mozart's time. There is often a great deal more to understanding the music than merely understanding the relationship between the notes.

I used to think folk songs were silly. They'd sing about things like, "The old grey goose ate up the corn." But in music appreciation class we learned that songs like this were often sung as oral dance music. When the fiddler or bagpiper got tired (or too drunk to play), people would sing as music to dance by. The teacher played a recording of an Irish folksinger who sounded for all the world like a bagpipe! I was astonished. Particularly when I heard her actually singing, "The old grey goose ate up the corn."

Popular Music

Understanding popular music isn't different from understanding the classic works. Rock and roll has a history, and the technical development of electronic instruments had important effects on the music that was written in this genre. Individual artists have impressed their style on the music, and cultural forces have affected what has become mainstream music and what remains cult music. We can apply everything we said about the technical mastery of classical music to the understanding of popular music. The more you know about popular music, the better you can appreciate it for its unique qualities.

To illustrate this claim, we deal—only briefly—with the work of the Beatles. The Beatles' music evolved from a rock and roll, rhythm and blues beginning on three guitars and a drum to a complex mix of exotic styles and instruments. They have incorporated elements of the blues, rockabilly, Latin music, and reggae. In various records they incorporated harmonica, banjo, flute, clarinets, Indian instruments like sitar and tampura, and the electronic synthesizer. They modified their music in the recording studio by taping over, "phasing," and running tapes backward or looping them. "Eleanor Rigby" incorporated a string octet. "Because" from the *Abbey Road* album is Beethoven's "Moonlight Sonata" backward with lyrics. And those are only a few examples of the technical innovations from the Beatles' albums. People who really study the Beatles and their music have a wealth of information about the performers, the music, the social background, and effects of this famous group. These fans experience the Beatles' music on a level of technical mastery that gives them an increased enjoyment that isn't available to the casual listener.

Mastery in Literature

Leaving the topic of music, we turn to the topic of literature. A technical mastery of literature is also the work of a lifetime, but we can begin in a small way as we did with music. To understand the technical aspects of literature, we also need to study the form of the work, the writer's life and times, and the history of the form and its relationship to other forms.

Writing Techniques We can study the techniques of play writing or poetry writing. We can study the history of stagecraft and the various ways space has been used to present plays. We can study the technical aspects of play presentation: setting, lighting, costume, and special effects. We can study how each of these aspects of theater affect the audience's perception of the play. We can study the various forms of plays: dramas, comedies, tragedies, farces, melodrama, and burlesque. What are the uses, the strengths, and limitations of each genre? We can study acting. What are the techniques of voice and movement that give the actor power over our thoughts and emotions? How are the illusions of thoughts and emotions created?

History and Development   We can also study the history of the theater in relation to the culture from which it has sprung. What did the plays mean to the people who first wrote them, acted in them, watched them? Knowing that the theater of Shakespeare's time had developed from the traditions of the popular morality and history plays as well as from the entertainments for the royal court can lead us to a better understanding of his plays. Some of his plays were written for the court of Queen Elizabeth I and some for the popular theater. The differences are striking, and an understanding of Shakespeare's purpose in each case can give a better appreciation for the plays themselves. We also need to know something of the history and political and economic conditions of England in Shakespearean times to understand what he was about. Did you know that women didn't act in plays in Shakespeare's time? All the female parts were taken by boys. Some of the humor is more humorous with that bit of knowledge.

We don't want to bore you with repetition. Quite simply, the more you know about a subject, the more interesting it becomes and the more you can appreciate the subtle and important distinctions that make a difference to experts. Knowing more about art doesn't take away from the simple physical appreciation; it simply allows you a deeper and more complex experience of that art. To listen for enjoyment on the level of technical expertise isn't something we will all undertake as seriously as the critics or the performers. But we can all learn more about what interests us and learn a different level of appreciation for what we already like.

Listening to Enjoy on a Level of Technical Mastery

To listen for enjoyment takes a serious commitment to study the subject that you are interested in. You must study the history and context of the literature or music in which you're interested, and you need an understanding of the technical skills involved in the creation and performance of the art.

AN EXTENDED EXAMPLE: *THE PIRATES OF PENZANCE*

In order to summarize what we have said in this chapter about listening to enjoy, let's take one example and illustrate how a single artistic experience can be enjoyed on all three levels of listening. As our example we take the popular Gilbert and Sullivan operetta *The Pirates of Penzance*. This comic opera was revived on Broadway and then made into a popular and successful movie. It's a good example to show how music and theater (and poetry, too) can be enjoyed by audiences at all levels of sophistication.

On the level of physical enjoyment, *The Pirates* is a wonderful romp. There are songs and dances, wonderful costumes and settings. The story is a simple one, but it has enough humorous twists to keep everyone interested. There are pirates and policemen and lovely ladies. The operetta has romance and adventure, fighting and singing. The hero Frederick, celebrating his 21st birthday and the end of his apprenticeship to a crew of pirates, discovers that he was supposed to have been apprenticed as a *pilot.* He decides to quit being a pirate; clearly it's his duty to fight them. Then he discovers that he isn't 21 at all; since his birthday is on the 29th of February, he's technically only five and a little bit over! He is still, therefore, apprenticed to the pirates. A paradox!

The pirate crew happens on a bevy of lovely ladies, all daughters of a retired Major General. The pirates capture the ladies, but release them when their father the General confides that he's an orphan. The pirates never rob orphans, a practice that's severely limiting their income since the whole area has learned of it.

The play is enlivened by many comic songs, sung to lively tunes. You whistle or hum Sullivan's songs long after you leave the theater. In one song, for example, the policemen confess that theirs is a hard life:

When a felon's not engaged in his employment,
Or manufacturing his felonious little plans,
His capacity for innocent enjoyment
Is just as great as any honest man's.
Our feelings we with difficulty smother,
When constabulary duty's to be done.
Ah, take one consideration with another,
A policeman's lot is not a happy one.

The comedy is compounded as the pirates sneak up on the Major General's house (they have discovered that he isn't really an orphan!) singing at the top of their voices and punctuating every line with a stomp of their feet:

With cat-like tread, (stamp)
    Upon our prey we steal, (stamp)
In silence dread (STAMP!)
    Our cautious way we feel. (STAMP!)

In the end, of course, the pirates surrender to the police at the mention of Queen Victoria's name. They sing:

We yield at once, with humbled mien,
    Because, with all our faults, we love our Queen.

The pirates are found to be fallen noblemen and marry all the General's daughters. The operetta has rhythm, rhyme, melody, harmony, and humor. You can listen to it just for fun.

As enjoyable as the operetta is on the physical level, it's still more interesting on the level of ideas. There is a good deal of parody and wit that's available for enjoyment to people who are aware of it. The whole play is a parody of the Victorian idea of duty, illuminated by paradox. If Frederick wasn't meant to be a pirate, it is his duty to defeat and arrest the pirates. But as an apprenticed pirate, he's duty-bound to help the pirates rob and pillage the countryside. There is also parody of the sentimentalism of Victorian middle classes. The fierce but tender-hearted pirates will not rob orphans and so are going bankrupt. Although they live outside the law, they are loyal to the Queen.

The Major General, father of the girls in this operetta, is a parody of a British type: the Military Man. He sings:

> I am the very model of a modern Major General;
>   I've information vegetable, animal, and mineral:
> I know the kings of England, and I quote the fights historical,
>   From Marathon to Waterloo, in order categorical.

And after some more nonsense of this sort, he confesses,

> When I have learnt what progress has been made in modern gunnery;
>   When I know more of tactics than a novice in a nunnery;
> In short, when I've a smattering of elemental strategy—
>   You'll say a better Major General has never satagee.

This verse and others like it allude to the fact that in the British Army there was a clear separation between the Officer Corps (who were all gentlemen and bought their commissions) and the Enlisted Men (who were commoners and did all the soldiering). There is another slap at middle-class pretensions through the General, who has retired, and become a part of the local gentry by buying a poor nobleman's house along with his lineage and ancestors. These are only a few of the many topical allusions in the operetta.

The rhymes are clever and puns abound. In the libretto Gilbert has played games with words as well as with ideas. Paradox permeates the play. The whole play is a parody of the popular melodramas of the time. There is a wealth of material that's available for people who enjoy the interplay of ideas.

And the play is interesting and enjoyable on the level of technical expertise, too. Sullivan, who wrote the music, was an accomplished composer who had an extensive education in classical music. He aspired to writing more serious music, but found writing for the middle classes on stage and in concert and music halls more lucrative. Sullivan knew many of the musical personalities of the time: Rossini, Clara Schumann, Johann Strauss the younger, and Jenny Lind, for example. Incidentally, Rossini was born on February 29, an interesting coincidence (or a paradox?).

Sullivan was a master at creating two different tunes for two different characters and then combining them in a counterpoint duet. In *The Pirates,* for example, he has the girls singing a song in 2/4 time ("How beautifully blue the sky") and joins that song with a song in 3/4 time by men's voices. In addition, the song changes keys from G major to B major and back again. Surely this is a technical mastery of the medium to be appreciated by people who know music.

And there are humorous parodies in the music itself for people who are familiar with grand opera. On the level of ideas the juxtaposition of the grand opera style of the music with the banal and commonplace rhymes of the libretto are amusing. But on the level of musicality there are still more jokes. The scene in which the Major General sings a solo while the police (hidden on one side of the stage) sing another song and the pirates (hidden on the other side of the stage) sing still another song is a parody of a scene from *Il Trovatore*, one of the more famous classical operas. And the song that the General is singing (surrounded by police and pirates) is modeled after a typical poetical address to nature of the time. Sullivan has provided a rippling orchestral accompaniment modeled after Schubert's "Auf dem Wasser zu singen." This is doubly sophisticated irony for the theater goer who also knows classical music.

The story of the production of *The Pirates of Penzance* is an interesting one as well, and knowing that story makes the play even more enjoyable. *The Pirates* was written right after *H.M.S. Pinafore.* That play was immensely successful both in England and in America. But in America the play wasn't protected under copyright, so Gilbert and Sullivan never got any money from its performance there. *Pinafore* opened in Boston on November 25, 1878, in San Francisco on December 23, in Philadelphia on January 6, 1879, and in New York on January 15. Within three weeks it was playing at five different theaters in New York. In all, there were over 150 different productions of *Pinafore* from which Gilbert and Sullivan received no payment and over which they had no artistic control. The quality of the productions varied greatly. So Gilbert and Sullivan decided to write an operetta specifically for the American stage to open simultaneously in England, to they could get paid for their efforts in both countries.

Gilbert and Sullivan contracted to open *Pirates* in December 1879 in New York. They sailed to America, arriving in November. But Sullivan had not yet written the music. He had sketched out the first two acts, but he left those sketches in London. So when he got to New York, he had to rewrite the whole thing. He was writing furiously to the last minute to complete the score (not an uncommon practice for him). Sullivan finally finished the score on December 27, rehearsed with the orchestra on the 29th and 30th, and opened on December 31, 1879! The play opened simultaneously in London, so Gilbert and Sullivan had copyrights to the production in both countries.

Knowing the story of the production and knowing the technical mastery of the librettist and the composer (of whose genius we have mentioned only a small example) make the enjoyment of *The Pirates of Penzance* richer. Listening for enjoyment on the level of technical mastery is available to anyone who wants to spend the necessary time to study the subject. But enjoyment of this operetta is also available to people on the level of ideas where the interplay of the language and the juxtaposition of music and words is also quite elegant. And anyone can enjoy the wonderful singing and dancing and humor of the plot.

When you listen to enjoy, you can set yourself a goal to listen on any or all these levels. Like Karl Haas, you can listen with the score or the manuscript on your lap to understand and appreciate the beauty of technical mastery of the medium. Or you can sit and listen and let your mind roam free to associate what you hear with whatever ideas come into your mind. Or you can simply tap your feet and hum along with the music or enjoy the drama or humor of the literature.

SUMMARY

In this chapter we talked about three different levels on which we can listen to enjoy either music or literature that's presented orally—plays or poetry. These three levels were: (1) enjoyment of physical sensations, (2) enjoyment of ideas, and (3) enjoyment of technical mastery. We illustrated how it's possible to enjoy any work of art on any of these levels. We also emphasized that none of these different ways of listening to enjoy is either better or higher than another; they simply coexist. You can set a goal to listen on any of these levels to enjoy listening to music or literature.

SUGGESTED ACTIVITIES

1. Attend or participate in a musical event. Pay particular attention to the physical experiences of the music or the play. Can you identify what physical elements of the music or language gave you pleasure to listen to? Attend a musical event that features music you are not familiar with. Do you still enjoy the same physical elements?

2. Attend a play or a performance of program music. What themes or ideas were presented in the performance? How did the characters or the plot contribute to the portrayal of those ideas? Or how did the music portray those ideas? Make a list of the ideas that came to your mind as you experienced the performance.

3. Read a selection of poetry. What themes or ideas were presented in the poems? What images were presented in the poems and how did those images contribute to the themes? Make a list of the ideas that came to your mind as you were reading the poems.

4. Check out a book from your local library about some aspect of your favorite music: about the composer, the artists, the history, or the instruments. After you have studied the book, listen to the music again. What do you hear now that you didn't hear before? Does the music have a different meaning for you now?

5. Check out a book from your local library about one of your favorite authors. Read about the author, the time period, the style, or the performance of that literature. When you have learned more about the author, how have the meanings you found in the literature before changed?

6. Check out a book about stagecraft or about acting. Read about how stage effects are done or about how actors achieve their effects. The next time you see a play, try to notice the technical aspects you have learned about. Does your new knowledge give you a deeper understanding of how the play works?

REFERENCES AND RECOMMENDED READING

Bacon, Wallace A. *The Art of Interpretation* (3rd Edition). New York: Holt, Rinehart and
     Winston, 1979.
Blair, Walter, and John Gerber. *Repertory: Introduction to Essays and Articles, Biography*

and History, Short Stories, Drama and Poetry. Glenview, IL: Scott, Foresman (1969).

Blume, Friedrich. *Classic and Romantic Music: A Comprehensive Survey.* New York: W. W. Norton, 1970.

Butcher, Philip. *The Minority Presence in American Literature 1600–1900.* Washington, DC: Howard University Press, 1977

Copland, Aaron. *On Music.* New York: Doubleday, 1960.

Forcucci, Samuel L. *A Folk Song History of America.* Englewood Cliffs, NJ: Prentice-Hall, 1984.

Gottesman, Ronald, et al. *The Norton Anthology of American Literature.* New York: W. W. Norton, 1979.

Haas, Karl. *Inside Music.* Garden City, NY: Doubleday, 1984.

Lawless, Ray M. *Folksingers and Folksongs in America.* New York: Duell, Sloan & Pearce, 1960.

Rich, Alan. *Classical Music, Orchestral.* New York: Simon & Schuster, 1980.

Russell, J. P. *The Beatles on Record.* New York: Charles Scribner's, 1982.

Sales, Grover. *Jazz: America's Classical Music.* Englewood Cliffs, NJ: Prentice-Hall, 1984.

Southern, Eileen. *The Music of Black Americans: A History.* New York: W. W. Norton, 1983.

Glossary

absolute music   music for its own sake; music that doesn't refer to particular ideas or feelings

abstraction   a word that has no concrete referent, as intelligence

acoustic cues   sounds that have meaning

analogy   a process of reasoning that like causes have like effects

argument   a claim supported by reasoning and evidence

backstage behavior   the way of behaving when no strangers are present

bandwagon   an irrational appeal to the desire to go along with the crowd

card-stacking   an unethical form of argument by presenting only positive evidence, while hiding negative evidence

cause/effect   a reasoning pattern that connects events in time

character   the people in a work of art

claim   a statement that someone wants you to believe

cochlea   the part of the ear that transforms mechanical energy of sound waves to electrochemical energy in the perception of sound

context   elements of the situation that affect communication

deduction   a process of reasoning from generalization to specific example

dual perspective   looking at a situation from another person's point of view

emotional persuasion   a persuasion focused on feelings

empathic listening   listening to discover the other's point of view

evidence   facts used to support a claim

fact   a statement that can be verified

form   the structure of a work of art

frequency   a physical property of sound

goal-setting   deciding what you want to accomplish

harmony   playing several notes simultaneously, such as in a chord

hearing the physical process of the reception of sound waves by the ear and brain

imagery the use of words to evoke physical feelings of sound, touch, colors, textures, and so on

incus a small bone in the middle ear

induction the process of reasoning from examples to generalization

inference a prediction based on experience

information the orderly arrangement of parts that form a code or system that has meaning for whoever uses it

inner ear the part of the ear from the oval window to the eighth nerve

intensity a physical property of sound

interaction a relationship governed by social rules

judgment a statement of preference

listening a mental process of interpreting sound waves in the brain

loudness a psychological property of perceived sound

malleus the small bone in the middle ear

melody the organization of notes into phrases

middle ear the part of the ear from the eardrum to the oval window

mirror question a question that paraphrases what you heard to check whether your interpretation was accurate

mudslinging the unethical form of argument by attacking another's character instead of replying to the issue

music theory the study of the technical and theoretical aspects of music

nonverbal communication communication without words, such as eye contact, facial expression, posture, touch, and paralanguage

norms unwritten and often unconscious social rules for behavior

onstage behavior the way of behaving when strangers are present

operational definitions concrete examples to illustrate and define abstractions

oral literature literature that's meant to be read aloud, such as poetry and plays

organizational patterns patterns of organization for messages, such as time, space, and so on

outer ear the part of the ear from the outside of the head to the eardrum

oval window the membrane separating the middle ear from the inner ear

paralanguage elements of the voice that are unrelated to words, such as tone, pitch, and so on

physical factors elements of the situation relating to external reality, such as light, temperature, and so on

physiological factors elements of the situation relating to internal physical sensations, such as hunger, fatigue, and so on

pitch a psychological property of perceived sound

plot the action in a piece of literature

program music the music that focuses on ideas and feelings

propaganda persuasion for the sole benefit of the persuader

psychological factors elements of the situation relating to internal feelings; interpretations of the situation

rational persuasion persuasion by logic

reality checking listening to discover what social rules apply in the situation or to discover another person's interpretation of the situation

reasoning pattern logic used to connect an evidence with a claim

rhetorical process the process of setting communication goals and analyzing and adapting to the listeners and situation

rhyme   using the same sound at the end of two lines of poetry

rhythm   the "beat" of music or spoken language

social factors   elements of the situation relating to the relationships between the people present

speaking and listening goals   specific and appropriate goals set to improve communication

stapes   the small bone in the middle ear

strategy   a conscious plan by which to achieve a goal

sympathetic listening   listening to convey concern for the speaker

syncopation   putting the accent on the second and fourth notes, instead of the first and third; gives a lively beat

testimonial   a false evidence resembling expert opinion

theme   the meaning in a piece of art

transaction   an intimate relationship governed by mutually negotiated agreements

validity   the extent to which a claim refers to real conditions, the truth of a claim

Index